393.0973 Young, Gregory W.
YOU
　　　　The high cost of
　　　　dying.

$19.95　　　　　　　　50546011330306

DATE			
JAN 18 1996			
FEB 06 1996			
OCT 2 - 2001			

The High Cost of Dying

The High Cost *of* Dying

A GUIDE TO FUNERAL PLANNING

Gregory W. Young

 **Prometheus Books**

59 John Glenn Drive
Buffalo, New York 14228-2197

Published 1994 by Prometheus Books

98 97 96 95 94   5 4 3 2 1

Library of Congress Cataloging-in-Publication Data

Young, Gregory W.
   The high cost of dying : a guide to funeral planning / by Gregory
W. Young.
      p.   cm.
   Includes bibliographical references.
   ISBN 0-87975-868-6 (cloth) — ISBN 0-87975-874-0 (paper)
   1. Death—Social aspects—United States. 2. Funeral rites and
ceremonies—United States—Planning. I. Title.
HQ1073.5.U6Y68   1994
393′.0973—dc20   93-41859
                                               CIP

Printed in the United States of America on acid-free paper.

Acknowledgments

I would like to take this opportunity to thank the National Funeral Directors Association, the New Jersey State Funeral Directors Association, and my many friends in the funeral directing profession who readily provided information that I am making available to the general public. These dedicated men and women have taken the lead in policing their industry against those who would abuse the consumer's trust. A special thank you to Gene Foley. He set high standards as a trusted family friend.

Dedication

To my grandparents Herb and Jane Weatherhead, and to my parents, Howard and Rita Young, who taught me the value of fairness.

And to my son, Christopher, whose love of learning makes his father proud.

Foreword

In 1867, a teenage boy named Elzy walked along the railroad tracks that ran next to his farm in Ohio. He was on his way to learn a very important skill. Having finished the farm chores, he walked several miles to "class": the lesson was informal and the teacher was not a teacher at all, really, but a student. Elzy went to him every day because there were no textbooks on this subject, and few practitioners existed. Elzy could not enroll in the formal class that his "teacher" attended, because he was too young. So, he watched, listened, and learned the best he could. What was he learning? Embalming.

Why would anyone go out of their way to learn embalming? I can not answer for my great-grandfather Elzy, but I *can* answer for myself. For over twenty years, I worked side by side with my grandfather and my mother, both licensed funeral practitioners. In 1987, I left the profession, suffering from a severe case of burnout.

My success actually brought on my departure. I performed my work with integrity, and took people's welfare to heart. Perhaps Elzy knew that embalming, the new procedure he had struggled to learn, would be the key to the modern American funeral. But he could never have imagined the complexity of the industry in the 1990s, or that his great-grandson would own three funeral homes and a state-wide cremation service. I was successful because my family taught me that it was important to be fair to those who sought my services. Many of my friends were funeral practitioners as well, who practiced as I did. These conscientious men and women make up the majority of those in the profession. But I was able to carve out a niche for myself in an area of the funeral business—cremation—that had always been a source of substantial profit for my competitors. I realized that a low-cost cremation was difficult to obtain from most funeral homes. After

7

giving this consumer problem some serious thought, I felt sure that a volume "immediate" cremation business could be profitable while providing for the basic needs of the family at a cost that would be one-half (and in some cases one-fourth) of that charged by my professional colleagues. I placed advertisements in every yellow pages directory in the most populated areas of New Jersey. Just think of it as applying "volume discount pricing" to the basic no-frills cremation at a time when most funeral directors were making *huge* profit margins on the more standard cremation service. I advertised and delivered a low price for a basic service not previously available to the funeral-buying public.

During my career as a funeral home owner and operator, I received a letter of commendation from the New Jersey Division of Consumer Affairs for my work with the Funeral Directors Association. I filed charges against one unscrupulous funeral director who eventually lost his license for defrauding the public. I also gave the attorney general information that was used against a fraudulent monument company, and when the occasion presented itself I spoke to groups seeking advice on funerals. I became involved in disclosing wrong-doing in the funeral business because, as an honest funeral director, I was angry at those who would exploit the public in circumstances of emotional vulnerability. I believe the funeral business is a noble profession if practiced properly. It cannot wait for the horror stories to surface and for legislatures to enact new regulations or empower the Federal Trade Commission, or for the states attorneys general to look into allegations of fraud or misrepresentation. Professional funeral directors must take the lead and do everything they can to police themselves. Every profession knows who the bad apples are; in fact, they have far more knowledge than do the outsiders in law enforcement.

I retired at forty-two with few regrets relating to the business of being a funeral director, funeral practitioner, undertaker, whatever you may care to call someone who sees to the final disposition of the dead. I thought I was away from it, but it's hard to escape the calls from friends and acquaintances who ask for advice on getting a fair deal in arranging a funeral. Then of course there are the conversations initiated by people who want to know, "What do funeral homes *really* do?" Since I was one of "them," I have no trouble revealing what "they" consider industry secrets.

Any businessperson will admit that the public's lack of knowledge about some particular consumer item or service can mean big profits to those who know how to take advantage. It is perfectly natural that most consumers know virtually nothing about many aspects of a funeral. During a lifetime, the average consumer will be called upon to purchase funeral services only a very limited number of times, and those instances may be many years apart. Understandably, the subject of funerals is not something most of us would normally choose to read up on in our spare time. To many people the topic is eerie, spooky, macabre, depressing, or something we just want to ignore until we have to face it. But when it becomes necessary to arrange for the burial or cremation of a loved one, there *is* no time. According to the National Funeral Directors Association, most funerals cost between $3,000 and $8,500[1]; with prices escalating annually, no one can afford to be anything but well informed about the practices, procedures, and costs of funerals.

Honest funeral practitioners have nothing to fear from this book. Unlike some sensational media stories, I have no desire to indulge in exposés or muckraking. I intend to offer an honest, straightforward view of this very difficult and emotion-filled process. I hope that my efforts will make the functions of a funeral home less mysterious to the public. The consumer will learn why a funeral can be so expensive and that, like any other type of business, funeral practitioners control only some of the costs involved. Surprising as it might seem to many, funeral directors can be valued allies in holding down costs by acting as the family's agent with cemeteries, churches, limousine companies, airlines, florists, newspapers, and a host of institutions and agencies. Honest funeral practitioners will applaud the public's interest in gaining a clearer image of what funeral home owners do to make their living. When a funeral is professionally managed, the director can justify each and every one of the charges on the final invoice.

To the dishonest funeral director I say this: you prey on the emotionally distraught; you exploit their ignorance and take advantage of their vulnerability in order to make money. If enough people learn about the various services, fees, and procedures, from reputable and authoritative sources, you will be out of business.

This volume is designed to be a helpful consumer's guide to arranging a funeral while at the same time avoiding unnecessary charges. For quick reference readers will find at the end of the book a summary of how to select a funeral director and how to make funeral arrangements. But I would urge all readers to spend time with the less tangible aspects of a funeral. The reason we have funerals in the first place is to fulfill deep psychological needs. Reading this book from the perspective of a consumer will help potential purchasers determine their needs and acquire advice on how those needs can be economically fulfilled. As a first step, write down what *you* think your funeral needs are; the ultimate key to saving money is knowing the available alternatives and asking for them.

NOTE

1. *Funeral Costs,* National Funeral Directors Association, Inc., 11121 West Oklahoma Avenue, Milwaukee, Wisconsin 53227.

Contents

12   The High Cost of Dying

1

The Funeral as a Consumer Issue

While completing the final preparations for this book, I paused to watch an evening news program—"Dateline" on NBC. The show was called "Grief and Greed: Consumer Fraud Where You Least Expect It." Reporters dealt with abuses in the funeral industry, particularly in the selling and prepaying of pre-need funeral arrangements.* It included lurid examples of how the unsuspecting can be ripped off after arranging for cremations. The program highlighted specific blatant abuses by individual funeral need suppliers.

This is nothing new. Every few years someone in the media "discovers" that the funeral industry is a good target for criticism. It is not difficult to understand why the abuse of consumers is so hideously attractive to the media, and saleable to the public. There are few things more repugnant than imagining grief-stricken people turning to a funeral home for help only to have their trust violated by someone cloaked in the mantel of professionalism.

It is important to remember that the funeral business is not unlike any other industry. There will always be unscrupulous people who abuse the rights of consumers for their own gain. I have no quarrel with reports showing lurid details of abuses within an industry, as long as the industry itself is accurately portrayed. I suppose such reports have their entertainment value, and I am sure they do heighten awareness, but for the most part they deal with isolated cases for the sake of sensationalism. Unlike such horrific accounts of abusing the public trust, my efforts are specifically designed to inform and to serve as a consumer

---

*This is the popular and much-marketed arrangement of funeral needs beforehand to be sure that one's wishes are met and the family is relieved of the burden of making such arrangements after the death of a loved one.

guide. When necessary, I will certainly identify the unquestionably illegal practices that sometimes occur. But what is far more important, you will be taught how to purchase the funeral of your choice at a reasonable price, from the average, honest funeral director.

Make no mistake, the biggest moneymaker for the funeral director is consumer ignorance. And why would anyone expect most consumers to be well versed about the funeral industry? In spite of the fact that death has been referred to throughout recent history in terms such as "inevitable" and "more certain than taxes," it is not something that the average consumer tends to think about. Yet often, the young, the survivors, find themselves in the position of having to make funeral arrangements at a time of mourning, emotional stress, and vulnerability. Once a death occurs, there is no time to analyze and assess services in order to make a wise purchase. To compound the problem, most of us have very little if any experience in this area. How many times does the average person arrange for a funeral? Assuming the average lifetime for males and females, any random consumer would expect to have to arrange funerals for his or her mother and father, and if the consumer is married, the spouse's parents become a prospect; thus we can probably count on four occasions for arranging funerals over the course of many years. As families get larger and older, the frequency of death will increase. But viewed conservatively, the average person can expect to spend at least $12,000 on funerals. Here is why.

What kind of dollars are we talking about? The news program stated that the industry is a "6-billion-dollar-a-year business." The funeral director's trade magazine *The American Funeral Director,* for June 1991, uses statistics from among its own membership to show that over 62 percent of all funeral consumers spend in excess of $3,000 on a funeral. The same publication states that the average adult funeral was $3,247.46 in 1990. It also shows that the percentage of consumers purchasing funerals costing more than $3,000 has escalated sharply. Based on my research, almost 70 percent of all funeral purchasers are now spending, on average, in excess of $3,500 per funeral.

Is the funeral director making more money? Operating costs (overhead, staff, motor vehicles, etc.) have certainly climbed sharply.* This fact is largely responsible for driving up the cost of funerals to consumers. This puts additional pressure on the funeral director to make a sale. But what the funeral director doesn't want to see happen is an erosion

---

*Facts about why funeral overhead is high and getting increasingly higher can be found on pages 101–103.

of the basic social values that drive the traditional American funeral. They are integral to its future. The end result for consumers is that the average funeral director is not likely to try to talk them out of spending money in the traditional way. The "traditional" funeral service is synonymous with a "full service" funeral: i.e., the purchase of a casket, several days' use of the funeral facility (for visitation and the service), and a variety of added services from the funeral director.

Is the funeral industry a big business? If this is any indication, Service Corporation International is a funeral service conglomerate trading on the New York Stock Exchange. How big is it? The corporation owns 674 funeral homes and 178 cemeteries distributed over thirty-four states and the Canadian provinces. Gross revenues were expected to reach $681 million in 1993. The earnings per share of stock were expected to rise about 12 percent and the dividend paid is definitely up.[1]

The corporation used sound business practices to purchase and consolidate the overhead of funeral homes, florists, cemeteries, and livery services. Ask yourself: If you set your sights on developing a billion-dollar corporation, would you choose the funeral industry? Large profits can be made on the consumer-driven full-service traditional funeral. If every person who died was cremated, there would be no selling of cemetery space. If the deceased were not viewed after death, there would be no need for expensive caskets or the funeral homes in which to display them. Respect for the body of the deceased and the traditional religious, social, and ethnic customs drive the need for the full-service funeral.

My point here is not to question or criticize the consumer's right to purchase a funeral that is as expensive or as inexpensive as the individual chooses, based on religious and psychological needs. I have no desire to change the values of the country in order to save money. I simply want to show consumers how to get the deal they want at the price they want to pay. This goal is important for two reasons and therefore this book is written on two levels.

1. This discussion should serve as a quick reference for anyone who needs specific knowledge about how to deal with a funeral director and how to make funeral arrangements. The quoted and estimated dollar values for items and services may change over time, but the basic guidelines will not.

2. This book can serve as a starting point for all who want to reflect on those aspects of the funeral that are important to their respective psychological and religious needs. For that reason it contains a reference bibliography suggesting sources of information on various

aspects of the death experience, the funeral, and personal resolution of the death experience for the survivors.

Regardless of what type of funeral is selected, I outline a plan that will hold down the costs. To develop ideas on what elements of the funeral are important to all consumers, I suggest reading this volume from beginning to end in order to encourage readers to think about the elements of a funeral that fit the needs of a given purchaser.

For those whose need for information is more urgent, use it as a quick reference source in order to get a fair deal: Read the "Funeral Arrangement Check List" on page 97, and at least chapters 6, 7, 8, and 9. If you are considering preplanning for a funeral, by all means, read the whole book. But however you come to utilize the information compiled here, before making use of the knowledge it imparts to actually deal with a funeral supplier, you must make yourself aware of how you fit into this category of "need."

1. You want the traditional funeral your family has always had, but you want to assure yourself that you are not being taken advantage of by the funeral supplier.

2. You want the traditional funeral your family has always had, but you want to change parts of it that are no longer meaningful for you, and you know that by doing so you will affect the cost.

3. You want the simplest and least expensive method of disposing of the person who has died. You can, if you choose, do something meaningful that suits your psychological needs after that disposal has taken place. In deciding where your consumer thinking fits, bear in mind that there may be others close to the deceased who have special needs as well. Are they important to the decisions made about the funeral?

NOTE

1. *Standard New York Stock Exchange Stock Reports,* Volume 60, Number 10, Section 26, January 15, 1993.

2

The Funeral in History

Several years ago I went to New York City to see the exhibit of the artifacts of Tutankhamen. This boy pharaoh, one of the less important rulers of ancient Egypt, gave to the world the most complete view yet of that country's ancient culture. The Egyptians believed that the pharaoh needed to travel with the implements of life for a successful journey to the other world. The mere fact that I was viewing man-made items crafted around 1300 B.C.E. amazed me. There were large items, including statues, alabaster jars, the huge sarcophagus that held the burial casket, and so on. We have all seen artist's renderings of thousands of people building the pyramids and dozens more moving the items into the tomb. But what held my attention the longest was a gold belt buckle. It would have been suitable for use today. Intricately crafted, it showed great detail. I remember being fascinated by the fact that this item was crafted by one person, not thousands. In looking at this gold belt buckle, I could picture the jeweler hunched over a table with his tools; I could picture him making each cut. I could relate to him. The thousands of workers moving the quarry stones and rolling the sarcophagus were faceless to me. But here was a single man's effort. Was he much different than me? I think not. He worked, supported a family, owned a home, and practiced his religion. I could picture him getting frustrated because he could not get one corner just right, and I wondered if he put the piece down, went home, and played with his kids.

Several days ago I was glancing through a *Life* magazine dated November 1991, when I came upon an article titled, "Hunter from 2000 B.C." There were pictures of a hunter who had died a thousand years before Tutankhamen, frozen in a glacier and now exposed to our modern gaze. He was found complete with clothing, hunting weap-

17

ons, and personal belongings. A quote from Stuart Needham, British Museums Curator of Bronze Age Antiquities, struck me. He said that there are plentiful graves from this era, "but gravegoods are conditioned by rituals of burial—this is our first look at real life."

That is an important statement. How a person is buried does not always reflect how the person lived. In many cases we feel the need to give the deceased more in death than he or she may have had in life. The same spiritual, religious, and psychological needs felt by man 4,000 years ago shape what we do with funeral practices today. There are few cultures in the world which lack ceremonies and rituals surrounding death. Belief in an after-life is a common theme. Are we so different from Tutankhamen? Ancient Egyptian religion dictated that his subjects prepare him for his second world after death. Many in our culture spend their lives believing they are living in a way that prepares them for their life after death.

Those who survive the deceased often believe that there are necessary religious rites that must be practiced after a family member dies. I will discuss in a later chapter the most common religious teachings in our society and how they affect funeral costs. For now, my purpose is to show that humankind has always felt the need for funerals of one type or another. These religious reasons for disposing of bodily remains can be traced through an organized religion's liturgy and teachings. But the need for ceremony runs much deeper than church teachings. To paraphrase the social commentator H. L. Mencken, "If there were no God man would find a need to create one." As thinking beings we perceive ourselves as having a permanent place in the universe. Perhaps it stems from the inability to accept that our existence is solely on this earth and even then for a limited period of time. Maybe it is our sense that we are a small part of the whole and will go on. Whatever the answer, the need for perpetuity is there in most of us in one form or another.

Early humans lived in a world of fear.[1] When they did not understand the natural phenomenon surrounding them they attributed events to the will and intentions of "spirits." The lightning that would result in occasional deaths could not be accounted for. A falling tree must have killed the child for a reason. Early ceremonies were attempts to protect the living from the spirits which it was believed caused the death of the deceased. Authors Stub and Frederick go on to say that the Polynesian word "tabu"—later corrupted by our modern culture to form the word "taboo"—meant "the condition of a person or thing set apart and shunned for religious purposes, also to excite horror, fear, and disgust." This taboo extended to the dead human body. The ancients often had their priests dispose of the dead body since they were emissaries of the gods.

Almost certainly the first to practice embalming, or any form of preserving the physical remains, were the Egyptians. Embalming was *required* in Egyptian society. Burial could not take place when the Nile was at flood stage. But to not bury the dead resulted in more deaths because of plague and pestilence. Also, the Egyptians believed that, after being accepted to the otherword, the soul had to return to the body, which physically made the journey, and, therefore, the body had to be preserved. There is a lot of speculation about "lost techniques," but mummies show us exactly how the Egyptians embalmed, complete with the aid of a dry climate.

Embalming techniques make the modern funeral possible. Just as the Egyptians had different types of embalming methods and an array of different procedures that depended on the deceased's social stature, so, too, does today's American funeral director. But it was not always so well structured.

Culturally speaking, the United States is a comparatively young country. Relatively few Native Americans are left. When the Europeans arrived, they brought the customs of their heritage and the religion(s) of their respective mother countries. The first permanent settlements were those of the Catholics of Spain and the Protestants of England. It is not hard to imagine that in a new, harsh environment religion played an important role. At the time there were no funeral specialists. Life in those days was not as segmented and specialized. Nevertheless, like the Egyptians, there was the need to dispose of the deceased quickly. Health reasons did not permit a lengthy viewing, and, if it happened at all, such viewing was for a very short period. The religious aspect of the funeral was governed by the church. The body was simply buried in the quickest manner possible and then the religious ceremony became the central focus. That is not to say that embalming techniques were not available. In fact, blood circulation, the basis of modern embalming, was discovered in 1628. By the mid-1600s arterial embalming was practiced in order to preserve medical specimens.[2] As North America was being settled by European colonists, methods to preserve a body were definitely known. But the reason for preserving was not the same as for the Egyptians. It was to make viewing of the body possible—not to maintain the body for some after-death journey. Strong religious influences were also a fact. All that was required for the fashioning of the new trade of "undertaker" was for American customs to evolve and create the need for such a tradesman.

One of my favorite spots in New England is Woodstock, Vermont. An approach to the town is made on a narrow, winding road along a river. Just before entering the town motorists pass an old wooden building along the road. Above the door is a sign that gives the family name and says "Furniture Store and Funeral Director." I hope they never take it down in spite of the fact that a new funeral home was built behind the store. It is a great piece of Americana and gives an important piece of historical information to those not familiar with funeral directing. As people settled into towns they took their respective places as specialists in supplying goods and services. I am not a sociologist, but I would bet that a tavern with rooms over the bar was the first building in town, followed closely by a general store. Somewhat further down Main Street came the furniture maker. He would have been building for the locals as the town changed from a stopping point along a traveling route to a place to live. It does make one wonder: as people died there, how were they buried?

With the development of communities it became harder to bury a loved one in the backyard when a death occurred. The church was now the social center of the community, and through the church, ceremony became important. If someone's beloved grandmother died, it was important for people to gather to comfort those left behind and to hear the minister give her a proper send-off. Being able to identify where her body was buried and publicly acknowledge her importance to those she left behind was the rationale for maintaining community cemeteries. Instead of burying the family on the farm, now there was a place designed to serve as the final resting place for members of the community who had died and were buried together. Not unlike the tombs of ancient Egypt or the crypts of Europe, a departed grandmother needed a special enclosure for the burial at the cemetery with her husband, and a casket to house her remains. And who in the community was known for building such cabinets—or what we now call caskets? The furniture maker of course.

But wait, this is getting complicated. If I build the casket, somebody has got to place Grandma into it. Now who digs the grave? Grandma's sons are right in the middle of getting in the crop and it is going to rain. No problem. The new chair I was building can wait. Pastor Jones wants the funeral tomorrow. I'll have my assistant Edward dig the grave while I finish the casket. While I am at it, I'll build a second casket for future use. Might as well. I have to cut the boards anyway. Since I don't want to be bothered by people looking for furniture until Thursday, when the funeral is over, I'll hang a black ribbon on the front door to let people know I have changed hats and won't be making furniture for a few days. Of course, folks need to know I am handling the funeral and they need to know who died. I'll hang a ribbon on Grandma's door and dress in black until the funeral is over. That way, the men carrying the casket know who to follow.

What has developed is the town "undertaker." He didn't dream up a new service and advertise hoping to attract customers. He "undertook" to do the job no one else wanted. Is it any wonder that soon he had horses that sported black plumes and a special carriage for transporting the casket?

My grandfather died at the age of ninety-five. I worked with him right up until the end. In the lounge of one of our funeral homes hung a picture of him on a horse-drawn hearse. I still have the tack hammer he used to put the interior fabric into caskets. As far as I know, he never built a piece of furniture in his life. I knew him as strictly a funeral director. But *his* father had worked in the furniture store in Bodkins, Ohio, and picked up the trade of "undertaking" from *his* father. Think about it: Jacob settled in Ohio as a furniture maker in 1820. His son Elzy took up the family furniture business. On the side they were "undertakers." One generation later, my grandfather, Elzy's son, had become a "professional," licensed as a "Funeral Director." But how could we transform from furniture makers to funeral professionals in one generation? Probably the biggest catalyst was the outbreak of the Civil War in 1861. While America's Civil War decimated the nation, it did wonders for funeral directing.

Battlefield casualties raised new concerns about disposing of the dead. Until the mid-1800s, families lived and died in one town or community. The Civil War raised the possibility that a family member could die in another state. If the brother, father, or son wasn't buried in a mass grave out of necessity, he could be returned for burial in the family plot in his home town. How was that possible? In addition to the fact that railroads and elaborate roadways made transportation much faster, the technique to preserve human bodies had been around for years. Because America's social structure found people living and dying close to home, measures to preserve physical remains simply hadn't been practiced, except in medical circles, to preserve bodies for anatomical study. Beyond the demand of medical research, there was no need for the practice. During the Civil War, however, it was used in an entirely new market. Itinerant embalmers, mostly doctors, went to the battlefields and used arterial embalming to preserve bodies for shipment home. A whole new service was created. With it came a degree of "professionalism" not found in "undertaking" before the Civil War. This required specialization, knowledge of anatomy, and surgical skill. In one step, undertakers acquired a skill that set them apart from the furniture makers who preceded them. No longer could just anyone provide a casket, horses, and a special carriage. Now the job required very specific training. My great-grandfather Elzy must have seen the need, but I wonder if he was aware of his changing role: from provider of funeral goods to supplier of "professional services." I believe he did, because my grandfather, his son, conveyed to me a deep sense of professionalism, self-worth, and stature within the community. With the advent of modern arterial embalming, the furniture maker had become a "professional." To this point undertakering evolved in response to social need. The undertaker's services were dictated by the public. But, arterial embalming gave him options he didn't have before.

Before the modern funeral director could be viewed more as a professional and less as a supplier of merchandise, one more important aspect of the funeral had to change—the in-home funeral.

I remember graphically my one and only "house" funeral in which the viewing, visiting, and funeral service all took place in the home of the person who had died, rather than in a funeral home. The year was 1969. I had never been involved in a funeral in which the body was left inside the person's house. The whole event could only be described as a logistical nightmare. We lugged folding chairs, lecterns, flower arrangements, and of course the casket from the funeral home into the house. The funeral was for one of a pair of sisters and the survivor required that everything be done in the house, including the embalming. My grandfather gave me a knowledgeable grin before he and I started the job. By the time the burial took place two days later, I had a far deeper appreciation for the convenience afforded by a building designed to accommodate funerals.

There proved to be no way to get the casket into the living room without standing it on end. It posed no real problem so long as the casket was empty, but it was not very dignified when the funeral procession left with the body. Nonetheless, that was how we exited the house—with the pallbearers standing the casket on end.

I had never embalmed a body outside of the funeral home, but it was no problem for Grandpa, who simply dug out several wood boxes circa 1900 containing all the primitive equipment needed to prepare a body in the home. The operation took about three times as long as it would have in our funeral home. The pumps that circulated the embalming fluid were archaic and slow; and if that weren't bad enough, the modern equipment found in the funeral home could not be transported to perform an on-site embalming. Once in the home, great care had to be taken since there was no modern operating table available. This meant that the funeral director had to embalm the body on the bed where it was likely to be viewed by friends and loved ones.

During the funeral service there was not enough room in the living room (or what was called the parlor) so some of the mourners had to listen from the kitchen. We needed twice the amount of hired help because we lacked the conveniences we were used to. We had no elevator, no private halls, no parking lot, and no flower delivery area. Consequently, we found ourselves constantly moving folding chairs that had been brought in for the occasion.

The point of relating all this information is to communicate the fact that the American funeral customs took another giant leap forward in favor of the funeral director when *home funerals* gave way to *funeral homes*. With the advent of such homes, funeral directors had gone the final mile. They built facilities that accommodated all the funeral needs.

Initially these "funeral homes" were converted houses. The one I started in was a stately old mansion that had been built for a man who had run for governor of the state. My grandfather had bought it with his father in 1914. The four-floor structure housed Grandma and Grandpa in a large apartment on the upper floors. The commercial funeral home provided consumers with the warmth of a "home" setting, but none of the inconvenience that came with utilizing their own house for the wake and related services.

As these funeral homes became established, another phenomenon occurred. In rural areas where towns were small, one or two funeral homes sufficed. Residents usually had one or two churches and their culture was generally the same. In urban areas established neighborhoods often had their own funeral home. In our two-mile-square area this was the pattern:

Two Protestant funeral homes, one frequented by the more affluent while the other saw to the needs of middle-class and blue-collar families.

Two Catholic funeral directors, one Irish, the other Italian.

One Black funeral home operator—definitely the nicest building in the neighborhood. I remember he had a sign out front that one of the family members was a lawyer and would help settle the estate.

Within another mile were two Jewish funeral directors; one catered to the orthodox and conservative, the other to the reformed and the more religiously casual Jews.

These funeral directors played an important social role to their peer groups. A time of trouble found people turning to a person whom they perceived as sharing their values, someone they could trust. There is something very comforting about "returning home": frequently we were asked to place the wife in the same room where the husband's casket had been. I will have more to say about people's loyalty to the family funeral director later, in chapter 8.

The institution of the funeral home served one other vital purpose: it provided the convenience of "one stop shopping." Where once my grandfather had to arrange the details of the funeral with the family, then drive them to the casket supplier's showroom, then to the cemetery, my mother would simply complete the arrangements and walk the family downstairs to select a casket. After the family departed, Mother would begin telephoning the various suppliers. She had become an agent who handled all the details. The process of making funeral arrangements had shortened from what had taken more than half a day to about an hour and a half. The funeral director controlled the entire funeral, with the exception of the details the clergy required.

The families loved the convenience, as did funeral directors. But in answering the public demand for convenience, funeral directors had removed the public from the process. Once funerals were conducted outside of the home, death was no longer regarded as a normal part of life. An aging or sick relative was not as likely to die at home now that there were hospitals and nursing homes. Unlike years past, children did not witness the illness and death of aged relatives. Instead, the phone would ring and the survivors would learn of the death. The funeral home would then be called and later the family would arrive to make the necessary arrangements. The body was not seen until visiting hours a day or two after death (possibly several days if out-of-town relatives were expected). In some cases the body was not viewed. Families did not care to ask about the process by which the body was prepared, since the procedure was no longer performed in the home. They arrived at the funeral home at a determined hour and walked into a room where the body in its casket had been placed, flowers appropriately positioned, and chairs provided for friends. Family members would continue and often add to the services their ancestors had handed down, but they became isolated from the process. The funeral director handled everything, as their agent and buffer. The family only saw the end result. They were asked what services and goods they wanted to select from the "menu," and when they returned it had been done. I have always argued that funeral directors provide a valuable service by taking on all the complicated and time-consuming details for a bereaved family, thus allowing relatives and friends to mourn as they see fit. But what funeral directors also do in sparing the surviving family members from having to deal with such concerns, is to significantly reduce their involvement in the grieving process. By placing itself totally in the hands of the funeral director, the family in mourning does not know how embalming is accomplished, has little understanding of caskets, and does not deal directly with the cemetery. This is a relationship of trust, and as such, a family ignorant of its alternatives, or too trusting of the funeral director, is ripe for being misled.

In 1976, I designed and built a 10,000 square foot funeral home in a community sixty miles from my old family homestead. The building was designed for just one purpose, to house conveniently large numbers of people in their own private areas for funerals. It allowed my staff to move caskets, flowers, and bodies without the public seeing anything. I could park ninety cars on the property, put people in limousines under a covered canopy and direct them to a casket sales room that offered a wide selection of styles, models, and prices. This marked a high point for me as a funeral director. I also believe that the mid-1970s proved to be the high point for the traditional funeral. We funeral directors had answered our customers' "needs." We were beginning to enter an age of increasing consumerism and eroding social and religious values. My funeral home garnered a lion's share of the area business because I offered convenience and the right attitude. I catered to people's wishes rather than trying to push them toward the traditional funeral customs. I saw my job as one of service and I knew that if I did it well, the business would be profitable.

Other funeral directors saw their sale in another light. A family ignorant of the available funeral alternatives was easily sold. With the bewildered and grieving family on the funeral director's turf, he can choose to offer only alternative services that profit him. If those who are purchasing the funeral do not know what questions to ask—if they neither understand the process nor know the alternatives—they are sitting ducks. Read on and I am confident that the odds of receiving fair treatment will begin to swing back in the consumer's favor.

NOTES

1. Clarence G. Stub & L. G. Frederick, *Principles of Embalming* (Dallas, Tex.: Lawrence Frederick, 1970).

2. Ibid.

3

The Funeral Director:
Why Would Anyone Want this Job?

When I retired from funeral directing I was averaging two migraine headaches a week. I was administrating two funeral homes seventy miles apart and a statewide cremation service. It was the type of job that requires a significant amount of self-satisfaction from anyone who chooses to pursue it. I was dealing with people who understandably did not want to be in the position to use my services (or anyone else's), and who, if I did my best job for them, would never know the problems I overcame to please them. Of course I had to always look my best and be the paragon of decorum while holding it all together in the emotionally charged arena that surrounds most deaths regardless of the circumstances. Every day was like Christopher Columbus arriving back from a strange world having lost his flag ship and half his crew but being told by the people who hired him, "You did an okay job, but where did you find time to get the tan?"

If you are a funeral director, it also helps to be slightly schizophrenic. A good professional director must have great sensitivity to be able to anticipate families' needs. He is part psychologist who shifts his emotional transmission into "calm" while in the public areas of the funeral home. In the back rooms he shifts into high gear, always on a tight deadline for everything and never knowing when he will get more business, which could totally disrupt his plans for staff and equipment. His is a crisis-filled, time-sensitive environment.

There was an advertisement on television several years ago about an insurance company that keeps switching hats. It illustrated fire coverage by wearing a fireman's hat. Then the switch was made to a yachting cap, then a construction hard hat. The funeral business is the same: first, the funeral director is an interviewer and counselor, eliciting information from sometimes emotionally distraught people; then he becomes the resource center, offering the family options that will satisfy their stated (and/or unstated) needs. Whether he admits it or not, the funeral professional is a salesman, but the client is unlike most "customers." Picture opening the door for people you have never met before and the first communication is a widow's uncontrollable weeping which continues for several minutes.

Now, switch hats and become these strangers' confidante. For instance, you are asked, "What do we do about the first wife, who wants to come to the funeral? My son says that if she does he will kill her, but she is insisting on coming." Or you ask the husband of the deceased for their marital status and he blurts out in front of the children that they were actually never married those forty-five years they were together. (Under the law he does not have the legal right to make funeral decisions in states not honoring common law marriages, even though they lived as husband and wife.) Now spend the next hour and a half ironing out their questions and problems while they wrestle with their new-found emotions of loss or maybe do not even realize yet that death has occurred, and they are just going through the motions.

When the family has left, it's time to develop the skin of a rhinoceros and make what they wanted happen: by two o'clock the next day move the person from where death occurred, embalm, dress, and present the deceased in the casket with a new hair style.

The church must be called to arrange for the service, the cemetery has to be contacted to open the grave, pallbearers must be selected, a limousine and flower car scheduled, and the death notices must be inserted by phone into three newspapers. Of course you have to chase down the doctor to sign the death certificate and, naturally, today would be his day off: there is no point to going to the Registrar of Vital Statistics to get a burial permit until the doctor signs.

While doing this the phone rings and it is another "first call" from a new family who needs to make arrangements. You have to do that one, too, because your entire staff is out running the funerals and they are not available. You have just sat down with the new family when your secretary, who has instructions not to disturb you while you are making funeral arrangements, informs you that a death has occurred and the police are on the scene requesting that the body be removed from the house. Of course that job takes two people to accomplish.

You do all of the above perfectly. The next day you open the paper only to find that they left out the mother's and father's names in the obituary even though you have it right on the information you gave to that paper. Everything is ready for the family to see the deceased for the first time but the flowers fail to arrive until after visiting hours start. No matter how small or large the funeral home is, these events are common. If funeral directors had enough staff to cover every eventuality, they would be out of business because the next week they may not conduct a single funeral!

It is not coincidental that many funeral businesses have been passed down through the generations of a family. In fact, nationwide, 84.9 percent of funeral homes are family-owned with that family having operated the home for forty-four years.[1] Why would anyone want to be involved with the care of dead bodies and the emotional trauma of their families? The most obvious answer is, that some people take the business lifestyle for granted and have been around it all their lives. Whenever I hired staff my main concern was to find out what motivated that individual to be in funeral service. I was always wary of the individual who had no prior involvement with the business.

Funeral directors readily sort themselves out into two types. There are the management types who keep all of these juggled balls in the air simultaneously, and then there are the hired-help types who deal with one job at a time. The management types can make a great deal of money, often because their family had been involved in the business for a long period of time and had established a solid reputation in the community. Others may have purchased a successful business (and the reputation that went with it) or developed one from scratch, in which case the essential community ties and professional rapport are nurtured and mature.

The hired help play a supporting role to the business owners and managers. They don't have the same opportunities for advancement or to make money that the management types have. Often, younger licensed funeral directors have seen the job as a chance to be involved in what they perceive as a profession. I have found that most were very sincere about what they were doing. My major concern has always been that they lack the training, education, sensitivity, or communication skills needed to be psychological counselors to grieving families. Consumers must use the funeral home staff for what this group can provide, namely a reference source for selecting options that suit the consumers' funeral needs. Those who plan and execute funerals are not psychologists, and even if they were, the short time spent making funeral arrangements does not give even a qualified psychologist enough opportunity to evaluate and counsel the consumer.

Consumers—the bereaved—must go to the arrangement conference with a good idea of what type of services they want. The funeral director can suggest alternatives once he understands what is wanted, but families should not look to him to design a funeral program that will fulfill psychological needs that only they can fully understand.

Functioning at his best, the funeral director understands the needs you the purchaser are communicating to him and suggests alternatives to achieve them. As a consumer you want a funeral director who is a trained "listener," not a trained "speaker." It is all right for him to make you aware of alternatives; it is not appropriate for him to try to sell you something you don't want or need. Your relationship to the funeral director should be similar to your relationship with an attorney. You must tell this professional coordinator and supplier of services what you want done. It is his job to get it done.

How are funeral directors educated, trained, and licensed? Each state sets its own requirements; there are no federal licensing regulations. There can be reciprocity between states, allowing licensed funeral directors from one state to perform some functions in another state. In general though, a funeral director must hold a license in the state in which he practices. It is possible in some states to be licensed as an embalmer, but not a funeral director. Persons so qualified can act as the preparer of the deceased but cannot direct the funerals. Once learned, the embalming process is relatively straightforward and routine. For this reason there were numerous "split" licenses. Cheaper help could be hired to prepare the deceased while funeral directors dealt with families.

With the onslaught of AIDS, increased regulation by various government agencies such as the Occupational Safety and Health Administration (OSHA), and new environmental restrictions, professionalism has become an important issue. As with everything else, the profession of funeral directing is becoming more and more complicated. Here credit must be given to the funeral directors themselves. They know that in order to serve a legitimate function, they need to increase their education and licensing requirements.

In order to find out what the licensing requirements are in each state, you need to know which state agency confers the license. This information can be found by contacting the agency that controls the professional boards that license funeral directors, by contacting the attorney general, or perhaps by inquiring with the Consumer Affairs Department. New Jersey, for example, requires at minimum an Associate's Degree, graduation from accredited funeral service school (usually a one-year, full-time course), the passing of a State Board Exam, and service as a trainee under a licensed funeral director for a minimum of one year.

Funeral directing and embalming schools teach a great deal of natural science. As you can imagine, there is strong emphasis on anatomy, microbiology, pathology, and the specific communicable diseases (e.g., AIDS, tuberculosis, and infectious blood diseases). With the discovery of the AIDS virus, funeral directors spend a great deal of time being taught surgical techniques and health procedures that will protect both them and the public. The schools also provide basic courses in fundamental business practices and a brief introduction to the psychology of grief.

State licensing exams stress those laws of the state which govern disposition of the deceased, and usually include a practical embalming exam. Recently there has been a move toward required continuing education (e.g., awareness of new techniques).

What does a funeral director do during the work day? It was not unusual for me to be awakened at 3:00 in the morning by someone notifying me that a death had occurred. If the person died in a hospital, the body can remain there until the next day. If the death occurred at home, in a nursing home, or as a result of a traffic accident, it is likely that the person would have to be removed to the funeral facility immediately. For that reason, funeral homes have staff members on call twenty-four hours a day.

The funeral director tries to find out, in that initial phone contact, what services are anticipated and when the family wants to come to the funeral home to make arrangements. He is already juggling schedules to accommodate them. The preparation of the deceased can take place before or after the funeral arrangement conference.

At the conference the funeral director is concerned primarily with three things: that the person who makes the arrangements is legally entitled to do so, that he can accommodate the wishes of the person outlining the arrangements, and that he will be paid in a mutually agreed upon manner. He must be certain that the paperwork complies with all state and federal regulations. At that point the family leaves and the funeral director must translate into reality what is on the arrangement contract. Throughout the conference the funeral director must assume that the person making the arrangements is giving factual and true information. The vital statistics that the funeral director uses to complete the death certificate and burial permit cannot for the most part be verified by him. He knows what legal paperwork must go to the state, the veteran's, and the Social Security administrations, but he has no way of knowing if the person giving him this information is being accurate, or even if the person is entitled to authorize the funeral. It is not unusual to have a person claiming to be a spouse come from out of nowhere after the funeral arrangements have been completed. On one occasion I actually had the dead man's two separate families sitting on opposite sides of the room, looking at his casket. I covered all the legal bases by having both wives sign the funeral arrangement form.

Most likely the funeral director, or some designated staff member, will immediately begin the process. A release must be obtained for removal of the body to the funeral home. Before any visiting hours can be scheduled, the service provider must know that there is time for all necessary prior preparations. Newspaper notices cannot be published until the designated clergy has verified service times. There must be enough lead time for the cemetery to open the grave site.* Each component hangs on another and every funeral director's nightmare is to have a glitch after the newspaper notices have invited people to calling hours or to a service. In accomplishing these functions, the funeral director is the family's agent and performs a valuable service. It is his knowledge in dealing with these various elements that can potentially save the consumer considerable amounts of money. Remember, he does not mark up (make a profit from) cash advances or monies paid directly to cemeteries, churches, and limousine services. The funeral director wants to get you the best deal he can. In performing these functions he is saving consumers the headache, anxiety, and heartache of having to deal with such unpleasant details at a time when grieving families are ill-equipped to manage. This allows the family to concentrate on what the funeral is all about, *mourning the loss of a loved one.*

Once the associated elements of the funeral have been put in place, the funeral director must now switch hats again. It is time to prepare the body for disposition, via either cremation or burial. If there is embalming, he will use surgical techniques to allow the deceased person to be viewed in the most comfortable and hygienic conditions (see chapter 7). The techniques can go far beyond simple arterial embalming. Many times I spent hours restructuring the face of an accident victim. It takes years of training to learn how to use suturing techniques to close wounds, and then to mold wax, much like a sculptor would, to hide the stitches. A good embalmer can sculpt any feature—an ear, a nose, or the lips—

*Please see the sample arrangement contract form on pages 52 and 53 to gain a better understanding of how many factors are involved in the average funeral.

and then expertly apply makeup to present a face that looks untouched. If the head and face are significantly damaged, measurements can be taken of remaining features to construct new ones. All facial features bear a measurable relationship to one another. For instance, the nose is a measurable distance from the ears, and the size of each facial feature falls within a measurable range in relation to the other features. Forensic pathologists use these measurements as a matter of course to reconstruct facial features from skulls. Seeing the parents of a child who went out of the house happy and was later struck and killed by a car, being able to confront the death by having an open casket reinforces the funeral director's sense of professional self-worth. Medical doctors experience this in the responses of their patients; funeral directors see it in the responses of the grieving family and friends.

Having prepared the body for viewing, the funeral director now sets up the rooms where the calling hours and/or the service are to be held. The small details the family has requested are now put in place. It's time to switch hats again and become the family's greeter and representative as people arrive to pay their respects. Whether he is at the funeral home, the church, or the cemetery, the funeral director is a diplomat who anticipates problems and smooths over squabbles. He is responsible for getting the funeral to where it is going on schedule. If the job has been done correctly, the family will never know that the casket delivery truck broke down fifty miles away, that the body wasn't released from the hospital until the last minute, or that the cemetery opened the wrong grave. Each of these details is handled in a supercharged emotional atmosphere.

It sounds as though a professional able to do this kind of job should command major fees for his services. That is not necessarily the case. The difference in compensation paid to management versus the supporting staff is enormous. The owner of a small firm with virtually no staff can do quite well if he is willing to devote every waking hour to his business. The owner of a large funeral home or a firm with multiple locations can make big money, but then again he has huge overhead and tremendous responsibility. The employee makes considerably less: with their "traineeships" and "apprenticeships," some firms resemble feudal trade guilds.

The truth is that funeral homes have seen a steadily declining profit margin due to increased overhead costs: many make less than 9 percent pretax profit. While the average cost of the funeral increased 67 percent to the consumer in the last decade, the costs of operation to the funeral home owner jumped 81 percent.[2] A newly licensed funeral director could probably make more money driving a truck. I polled my friends in the business and found that the newly licensed funeral director is hired at a salary of about $25,000 a year. Veteran licensed staff, not holding an interest in the business, can make up to $45,000 a year, and with exceptional talent incomes could reach the $60,000 mark. These figures are for New Jersey. Truck drivers can make $10 an hour, or just about the same as a starting licensee.

NOTES

1. *American Funeral Director* (June 1991). This is a publication of the National Funeral Directors Association.

2. *1990 Survey of Funeral Home Operations*, National Funeral Directors Association.

4

How Can the Funeral Director Help You?

If I had a dollar for every time I have been asked the following question, I would never have to work again: "The funeral cost X dollars. Did I get charged too much?" My response is that I have no idea until I look at the arrangement contract, *after* I talk to you about what goods and services you wanted.

The whole point of a funeral is to dispose of a deceased human being in a manner suitable to those who are responsible for the disposal. At one end of the spectrum is the simple, straightforward task of disposing of the body; there are no emotional concerns involved and the expense is kept to a minimum consistent with legal requirements. The other extreme is represented by a deceased person who meant a great deal to a lot of people, or perhaps to just one person. Those who are left have deep psychological needs which must be met.

In 1969 a landmark book was published. Elisabeth Kubler-Ross gave us *On Death and Dying*. One of the things she did was to name emotional stages that correspond to an individual's confrontation with the fact of dying. They are well worth repeating here because they parallel the emotional state of those making the funeral arrangements. The book is beautifully written and with great sensitivity. I recommend it for anyone interested in understanding grief and the psychology of coming to terms with death.

The five steps are: Denial and Isolation, Anger, Bargaining, Depression, and Acceptance. There have been other studies since her breakthrough publication and the stages have been expanded, but for our use her initial presentation will suffice.

I have observed people attempting to make funeral arrangements who were experiencing one or another of the five stages to some degree. Perhaps the most common is the first, "denial." I choose to apply it to the funeral and say that often people make funeral arrangements when they don't yet fully comprehend the death that has occurred. And that makes sense.

If a person dies in the hospital or in a nursing home, a phone call is placed to the survivor informing him or her of the death. The next question is usually "What funeral home do want us to call?" (In many cases, the name of the funeral home was required prior to admission.) If prior arrangements have not been made, the survivors, in shock from the news—or at least taken aback by the question— are often at a loss to reply.

I remember vividly one widow who described to me how her husband had been stricken with a heart attack while on vacation. He was placed in the hospital, where she remained with him for several days. She was told he was stable and that she should get some rest. Upon returning to the hospital, she was greeted by a nurse who had the yellow pages in hand open to the listing for "Funeral Directors." She was advised that her husband had died and to make the necessary call to have his body removed. Just moments after becoming a widow this woman found herself going through the motions of finding a funeral director. When she came to see me two days later, the funeral home that had removed her husband from the hospital and shipped him by air to us had been our only contact. As she sat in front of me it became obvious that she still had no true realization that her husband was dead. When she last saw him he was alive and talking. Physically exhausted from the return trip and the confusion of the situation, she had not yet confronted the death on an emotional level. She and her minister sat in front of me. I asked her if it would be all right to speak to the minister outside.

I told him that she was totally "flat" emotionally, and he, too, voiced his concern about her emotional state. He described her as being distant when referring to the actual funeral arrangements. We agreed that because she was accompanied by him, it was wise to give her the chance to confront the death by seeing her husband for the first time before she made the final arrangements. He had been shipped to us fully dressed and in a casket. All we needed to do was place him in a suitable room and touch up the makeup. I selected a small room off a larger room so that she would see the casket from a distance as she approached it rather than entering to find herself on top of it. With the minister on one arm and me on the other, we walked her through the large room toward the open casket. She totally broke down before we ever reached the casket. We placed a chair next to the open end of the casket so that she could sit there for a while.

After being with her for several minutes, the minister left her and joined me outside to wait. She sobbed uncontrollably for many minutes, then she became quiet and we could hear her talking quietly. Several minutes later she left the room and joined us.

There was no surer way for her to reach the understanding that the death had occurred than to expose her to it. When she confronted it she knew it to be a reality. Perhaps the most pronounced stage I saw in her from that point on was "anger." This anger was focused on the way she had been told that he had died, on being forced to conduct funeral business that she wasn't ready for, and at her husband for leaving her. For this woman the funeral experience became the beginning of the stages of grief, not the start of "resolution" or the return to a normal life after passing through the stages. Often people have the funeral service and are well on the way to resolution at its conclusion, perhaps having touched only briefly on some of the five stages.

Recently there has been a movement by some funeral directors in the forefront of their profession to enter into the field of grief counseling. Some funeral director associations have offered courses on the subject, training actually leads to additional professional credits. Since in some states not even a high school diploma is needed to obtain a funeral director's credentials, the thought of these individuals attempting to counsel a grieving person is in my opinion ridiculous. (I think of the widow who used to call us three years after her husband's death and ask us what to do. Her husband was "in the kitchen" and she was confused because he wouldn't eat what she cooked for him.) I do not believe that funeral directors should do more than they are qualified to do, namely, see to the burial of the dead and sell related merchandise and services to achieve that end. Ethically, we have an obligation not to take advantage of people in the delicate emotional stages of grief. But therapy is best left to qualified professionals. Our contact with clients is limited and transitory.

This places the funeral director in a position of supplying goods and services to people upon request. No one has the right to tell another how much to spend and what quality of funeral to purchase. Different cultures and religions require different goods and services. Individual tastes and desires vary greatly. It is a part of the mourning process. I condemn the consumer advocate who does not understand peoples' needs yet pushes the least expensive way out on the survivors, and I loathe the funeral director who preys on a survivor's guilt in order to sell a higher-priced package of goods and services. A funeral director who does his or her job with integrity wants to know what a client's needs are in order to satisfy them. If that means recommending a less expensive casket that will serve the same purpose, then so be it. In the long run, integrity is good for business. I learned early that word-of-mouth from past clients results in referrals.

If a funeral director's job is to provide goods and services to help individuals cope with the loss of a loved one in a manner suitable to their requirements for mourning, how does he or she accomplish that job?

THE FUNERAL DIRECTOR ACTS AS AN AGENT

In today's society burying or cremating a body is not uncomplicated. Funeral directors are licensed by the individual states because there is specific knowledge required in order to legally remove a body from where the death occurred, prepare it for burial or cremation, and see to that final disposition. Death must be pronounced by a proper authority; the death certificate must be signed by a medical authority legally entitled to do so; and preparation of the body must be performed under legal, medical, and sanitary guidelines. Formal records of the death are filed for permanent placement with government offices. In addition to having to know the legal requirements, funeral directors have to understand a variety of social and religious customs. Life is just a bit more complicated than when great-grandpa Elzy learned embalming in his spare time.

The funeral director can not act as your agent in a proper manner unless three conditions exist:

1. The funeral director has to have your interests at heart.

2. The funeral director has to know how to elicit from you what your desires are.

3. The funeral director has to know *all* the alternatives available from which you can choose *and* present them to you.

Now that you know how the funeral director can help you, it is time we turned to the heart of this book: How do you know what you want and need, and how do you get it from him?

5

Burial or Cremation?

There are many options for disposing of a deceased person, but they center upon two alternatives, burial and cremation. When taken alone, the cost of either form of disposition is minimal. It is the costs of the attendant services and merchandise that increase the total expense of a funeral.

Burial is the most common method in America for disposing of human remains. However, cremation is gaining in popularity. In-ground burial is still the most common, but "above-ground" interment in mausoleums is on the rise. It is not difficult to trace back four or five generations to our European ancestors who settled in North America to understand why in-ground burial came to be the choice. It was quick, effective, and it could be accomplished anywhere. In-ground burial also suited the customs of Europe. A grave could be marked for memorialization.

IN-GROUND BURIAL

Today burial is done, for the most part, in dedicated cemeteries. In some places you can still bury outside of cemeteries as local and state law allows, but generally we have to deal with cemeteries, which have requirements regarding burials.

The first requirement is establishing the proper ownership of the plot. If ancestors are buried there, who did the right of ownership pass to? Does Aunt Tilly have the right to bury her husband next to the original owner of the plot, or does her sister have that right? There are only two graves remaining and six family members; someone will be left out. In general, there was a deed issued at the time of the original purchase. The direct descendants have the right to perpetuate the use as governed by the laws of survivorship for the state in which the burial will take place.

It is the funeral director's job to contact the cemetery with the proper family information and establish that the deceased person has a right to be buried in the designated plot. The cemetery will often require the original deed, or they have in their records who the survivors are and the names of those who are entitled to make use of the plot. The cemetery will often tell the funeral director which member(s) of the family must sign the burial authorization form. In older cemeteries a funeral director may go the plot with a member of the family and a representative of the cemetery to identify a location. Regulations can be very tight or very loose depending upon who controls the cemetery or who manages the facility. There are no federal laws controlling cemeteries. As is the case with funeral homes, the states provide whatever regulations are needed to govern the use of cemeteries.

Once a grave has been selected, it must be opened. Usually the cemetery has someone retained to do that job or has full-time employees for the purpose. Sometimes the funeral director does the hiring.

Grave openings can either be "single," "double," or "triple" in depth. Single allows for only one body per grave opening; double means one on top of another; and triple places three bodies in one vertical opening. If a concrete or metal "burial vault" is used, it is generally no problem to reopen a grave and place another casket on top. If no vault is used then generally the grave cannot be reopened to place another casket in the same grave site. Cemeteries have various combinations of charges to affect these interments. Here is an example:

single-depth grave opening	$325
double-depth grave opening	475
use of a wooden outer box instead of concrete	75
move headstone foundation	125
install new foundation	225
deed transfer fee	150
perpetual care (generally a one-time charge for maintenance of the grave site)	200
back care charges (accrued charges for unpaid plot maintenance)	500

Cemeteries make money in two ways: they sell grave space and they utilize it after it is sold. If a cemetery has sold out its grave space and is living off grave openings and continuing charges, there will be "creative" charges beyond the simple grave opening. It is the funeral director's job to secure for his clients the best utilization of that cemetery space. For instance, you would probably not want to bury a person single depth in a grave allowing for double depth burial if there are more members of the family to be buried there. It is less expensive to reopen than to purchase. But, the person on the bottom must be in a concrete burial outer box, otherwise the grave can't be reopened. Is it more cost effective to go double depth and buy a concrete outer container for the casket than to buy a new grave alongside and only open it to single depth?

The funeral director routinely makes these recommendations to families. It is his knowledge of the particular cemetery, or his ability to ask educated questions based on knowledge of the burial practices, that can save clients money and inconvenience. He also is the one who will probably sell you the outer concrete burial container in the event that one is required.

If a grave is being bought for the first time, the family should consider several factors and ask numerous questions. Is the cemetery new or old? Newer cemeteries are not as likely to have higher charges at the time you need to utilize grave space in the future because they are still selling space. Older cemeteries have to make money on the utilization of the graves previously sold. What are the requirements regarding the individual burials? Is a concrete vault needed, and can graves be opened to double depth? How well kept is the property? Can any of the cemetery charges be assessed on a continuing basis (i.e., such as yearly maintenance fees)?

Purchase of cemetery space should be approached cautiously after fully considering your future needs. Today's society is a mobile one: how many of us live where we did ten or even five years ago? Is it wise to purchase grave space for family members who might never make use of it? On the other hand, if space is already owned, then thinking about maximizing the number of burials by interring the first burials in a manner that would allow for others to be buried on top starts to make some sense. Each family situation is special and unique. If a family is small, or if the survivors of a parent's death are young, it would make little sense to buy additional grave space on the assumption that in fifty years they would want to be buried there. Conversely, a sixty-year-old, unmarried only child would be perfectly justified in buying a third grave for himself next to parents who had just been buried. Keep in mind that one way to avoid high cemetery charges is to be cremated and have the ashes placed in a family plot.

ABOVE-GROUND BURIAL (MAUSOLEUMS)

A relatively recent trend is above-ground burial. In our society the wealthy have sometimes built their own small buildings within cemeteries to house their families after death. In older cemeteries they can be easily found with the family names inscribed. They were generally built solidly of large stones and mortar with closed niches in the side for the caskets to be placed. The entrances were guarded by locked bronze doors and/or gates. It is a simple matter to unlock the door and place a new casket in a vacant niche. Now this concept is available to the general public via large, group mausoleums.

It doesn't take a financial genius to figure out that a cemetery running out of grave space can make more money by putting 2,800 caskets in a building covering as much ground as is required to bury 800 caskets. The cemetery can sell the above-ground space for far more money than a below-ground grave and there is virtually no cost to open the mausoleum space for the casket. The expense to the cemetery is the cost of the building and the advertising necessary to sell it. The advertising would have the consumer believe that grave space is limited and that there are many advantages to the above-ground burial. Quoting from the brochure from a local cemetery, "Entombment in an above-ground mausoleum provides your loved one with a final resting place free from the unfriendly elements of the earth."

Grave space may very well be limited in some cemeteries, but it is not limited nationwide. The advantages to above-ground burial are mainly to the cemetery. Shown here is the cost at one cemetery of a mausoleum entombment compared to an in-ground burial:

	MAUSOLEUM	BURIAL
PURCHASE	$2,890.00*	$ 400.00
OPEN AT NEED	225.00	300.00
VAULT REQUIRED	0.00	400.00
HEADSTONE	0.00	450.00
TOTAL	$3,115.00	$1,550.00

*These prices represent the equivalent to inter and mark the place of interment. *Not* included is the fact that a sealed metal casket is required for the mausoleum. That will add at least $1,000 to the mausoleum cost represented.

At this juncture I have to make one point very clear: *The entire funeral industry is based on the premise that the consumer has psychological needs.* In my opinion, no one has the right to tell a grieving family that it shouldn't spend $3,000 to buy an above-ground mausoleum space, *if the family members fully understand what they are doing.* It is pleasant to sit in a chapel with stained glass windows and look up at the marble end plate of the mausoleum niche bearing a relative's casket. Is it more pleasant than standing at the graveside and reading the name on a stone while listening to the birds? Those are extremely personal questions.

One cemetery with which I have dealt many times has an amazing mausoleum. It was possible to buy a literal room where the interment of the casket takes place. The room could be furnished any way the owner desired. One room that I marvelled at contains the following: There is a table around which there are chairs. On the back of a chair at the head is a college letter sweater. On the table is an empty bottle of wine and glasses from which it was drunk. The gate to the room was locked in 1944 when the World War II flier was interred by his college buddies. I have been in another mausoleum that was designated as an air raid shelter for the city of Newark, New Jersey. The massive structure is granite and has several stories underground as well as above ground.

It is not surprising that some people seek above-ground burial not only for the memorialization, but also for the comforting thought that the burial is not below ground. Modern mausoleums are constructed in the following manner: forms are used to pour concrete in a "honeycomb" pattern, one niche on top of another stacked as high as the cemetery wants to go. Depending on the size of the mausoleum, niches can open to the inside into a central room, often used as a chapel or to house cremated remains, or it can open to the outside. When a casket is placed into a niche, the end of the niche is sealed. The sealing plate on some is fiberboard or plastic pressed into caulking compound. Over the front is hung a stone plate on which the person's name is generally inscribed. It is held on by a decorative fastener at each corner.

Mausoleum interment is expensive. The representative cost in the New York metropolitan area is anywhere from $1,500 to $15,000 to purchase, and up to $500 to open at the time of need. In addition, a sealed metal casket is required in most mausoleums. I will discuss merchandise in chapter 7, but a sealed metal casket means additional expense: buying a casket that has a rubber gasket and locking devices, for example. The reason that that type of casket is required by some cemeteries has to do with the mausoleum being vented to allow for the escape of gases that occur as a result of the decomposition of the deceased. Deodorant and air-venting systems are not uncommon in mausoleums with central rooms for the public. If you are considering mausoleum space, ask yourself some questions. Is it worth three to ten times the expense of in-ground burial? Is any building really "perpetual"?

CREMATION

Cremation offers an inexpensive alternative to in-ground or above-ground burial. It literally is the applying of extreme heat to the body to effect first, partial dehydration then burning. Cremation takes place in "retorts" which are the actual sealed chambers in which the process takes place. Crematoriums have varying rules regarding how the deceased is to be delivered to them. I have never dealt with a crematory that did not require that the body be in a container of *some type*. Cardboard is allowed as is "flakeboard" at some crematories. But this is likely to change as environmental laws become more strict. Since the gases from the process are vented to the outside, clean burning is becoming a concern. With the extreme heat, the compounds in glues used in fabricating burial containers are a concern to environmentalists. I required a rigid container to be purchased. These were available to the families for under $100. And I would not ask the funeral directors who worked for me to handle bodies that were not embalmed or in a proper container, regardless of what the crematory allowed. The cost of the actual cremation, with no other fees, can be as little as $130 or less.

Most people think of cremated remains as "ashes." Because of the high heat, the container (or casket) in which the body is placed has burned off, with one exception: the metal fastenings and handles do not burn. What the crematory is left with is some bone fragments and the metal fittings of the casket. What is commonly referred to as "ashes" is actually ground-up bone fragments with any other foreign matter removed. For an average adult, the remains fill a box about 12 inches by 4 inches. These processed remains are then returned to the family or the funeral director in inexpensive containers made of cardboard or plastic.

Many things can be done to memorialize the remains. They can be buried, scattered, or placed in urns for above-ground display. Many families have chosen to memorialize their loved ones by leaving them on funeral director's shelves for years! That is understandable, since cremation is regarded as a finality. If survivors do not feel the need to memorialize the cremated remains, the ashes are often forgotten. Cemeteries offer gardens for placement or scattering as do some churches. As far as law in New Jersey is concerned, cremation is final disposition. Within the bounds of environmental law, cremated remains can be scattered. In some states this can be done over public land or over private property. For instance, scattering cremated remains at sea is by far the easiest and least expensive way to bury at sea. You must travel beyond a designated mileage limit, the container must be opened so that the "ashes" dissipate, and a record must be filed as to the fact that cremated remains were disposed of in that manner. I have often placed cremation urns in a casket or buried them in a grave next to a casket. They can also be placed in a cemetery mausoleum. As a practical matter "ashes" are sterile and nonpolluting.

The consumer should look at cremation for what it is: an inexpensive alternative to burial. The services leading up to the act itself can be exactly the same as would take place before a burial, if the family's religious and philosophical beliefs can entertain the concept.

The average cost nationwide for an "immediate cremation" is $765.00.[1] We define an immediate cremation as the direct disposal of a deceased human being without any attendant services. It should be viewed as the most cost effective way to dispose of a decedent. To some people, services without the body present are sufficient for their needs.

A third alternative, sometimes sought, is burial of a casket at sea. This is a difficult and complicated procedure. Veterans of the service can be aided in doing this by the Navy, which will actually take a casket to sea for burial as part of its duties. There are very stringent requirements as to the preparation of the casket and places of interment. For our purposes here, suffice it to say that it can be done.

In learning the options of burial or cremation, you as the consumer have a better idea as to how the costs of these methods of final disposition can vary. It should have become obvious at this point that you must rely on the funeral director to present your options to you. You are now armed with some alternatives for what is the simplest part of the funeral. The services and casket you choose leading to burial or cremation will make up the bulk of your funeral expense. In the next chapter we will explore how you can spend either $500 or $50,000 on a funeral.

NOTE

1. *Funeral Costs,* National Funeral Directors Association pamphlet.

6

What Kind of Funeral Service Do You Need?

One of my funeral homes had an entrance with a long center hallway. On one particular morning, the largest room situated on the right side of the hall had five people in it. They were waiting to enter a limousine for the trip to church, then on to the cemetery—a drive of two hours. The bill for the funeral would be $7,475.

A smaller room on the other side of the hall also had five people in it. They were listening to a clergyman finishing the service. They would leave the casket at the funeral home and gather at the widow's house for lunch. The bill for the funeral would be $1,350.

In a third room, one of my employees was completing arrangements with five members of another family. They would leave and not be back. Their total bill would be $750.

Why are the prices so different? In the case of the first family, several days of visiting hours were scheduled at the funeral home. They had friends in the city where they had grown up and where the eventual burial was to take place, so they asked that newspaper notices be run in that community as well as in their current area of residence. They owned grave space in a cemetery, but the back care had not been paid for over twenty years. They were not concerned that the cost for this care totalled $350 and that the grave opening fee was $700. The family could have purchased a new grave in a nearby cemetery and opened it for much less than it would cost to use the old cemetery. Nonetheless, their decision was to return to the out-of-town location for the burial because that is where the rest of the family was buried. They had selected a sealed steel casket which cost $3,000 because the deceased had been an iron worker and appreciated metal work. And not taking the body into the church for the final service was unthinkable.

The second family had opted for a brief service in the funeral home.

They had wanted it to be private for the family and had invited friends to meet with them at the widow's house after they left the funeral home. The deceased had died at home (surrounded by his family) after a long illness. They saw no need to have an open casket. Because they wanted cremation, the family had selected the least expensive wooden casket available, but one that was still quite suitable for viewing at the service. Directly after the funeral, one of the funeral home staff would take the casket to the crematory. The ashes were going to be scattered offshore by the family because the deceased had been an avid fisherman.

The third family had completed arrangements for an immediate cremation. They were the nieces and nephews of a reclusive aunt who lived alone. They had sent her Christmas cards each year, to which she never responded. Her death was discovered by the only neighbor she talked to. It was the police who had called the family after finding the envelopes she had saved. The ashes were to be sent to the cemetery where her husband had been buried years before. There, they were to be placed at the foot of his head stone. The relatives felt that that was the proper thing to do, though she had not left any instructions.

What each of these families has in common is the fact that they have done what they felt they needed to do to take care of the final disposition of the deceased according to their relevant religious and psychological needs. The cost of the funeral is a direct result of three things:

(1) the funeral home's service of staff and facilities;

(2) the merchandise selected (e.g., casket, vault, etc.);

(3) the charges of outside parties the funeral home has contracted for, or "cash disbursements" made on behalf of the family.

The families are fictitious, but the types of services they purchased are typical of the services I performed every day. The analogy is designed to show the diversity of services and prices available if the consumer knows what to ask for.

By far the most inexpensive funeral is what I have called an *immediate cremation*. It is accomplished by arranging, in the most direct manner possible, to have the body transported from the place where death occurred to the crematory. It includes all the funeral director's services and staff, use of the facility for the casketing, and transportation to the crematory. In its simplest form it utilizes the least expensive receptacle available for the body. There is no viewing or visiting and no type of service. It is also referred to as a "direct disposal." With the exception of a stop at the funeral home to casket the deceased and the need to wait while the necessary paperwork is filed, that description is an apt one. According to a 1990 survey of funeral home operators, conducted by the National Funeral Directors Association, the average cost for this service in the New York metropolitan area is between $500 and $1,000 ($765 is the average cost nationwide).

As additional items are included in the immediate cremation, the cost mounts. If a direct burial is sought instead of direct cremation, the family incurs higher cemetery charges, perhaps the need for a better casket, and probably a burial vault. If we stay with an immediate cremation, it is not unusual to add newspaper notices, extra certified copies of the death certificate, and perhaps interment of the cremated remains. Now we can add a "memorial service" in which clergy officiate, but no deceased is present. It can be held in the funeral home, thereby incurring additional facility charges. Once I arranged to have the widow's limousine follow her husband's hearse to the crematory. She drove on while the hearse stopped to unload the husband's casket for the immediate cremation. She just wanted to travel the last mile with him. She incurred only an additional limousine charge, which was added to the immediate cremation minimum. The point is that she felt she had done exactly as he had wanted, and for an additional charge of $75, she was at peace.

Families should be well advised before opting for an immediate cremation. I am the last one to suggest an increase in funeral costs, but there is sound reasoning behind the opinion that sometimes viewing the body is beneficial. I share that opinion. Recall my story of the woman whose husband died while they were on vacation; she did not see him until several days later in the funeral home. As we all know, funeral ceremonies allow those who have suffered the loss to confront the stages of grief and move toward resolution so that a normal life can resume. There are occasions when the person who dies leaves instructions to the effect that there is to be no service. That decision should be left to the survivors. What do *they* need? Remember the remaining family of the reclusive aunt? They had an immediate cremation and added only the cost of interring the aunt's cremated remains. If they thought to send her Christmas cards, even though she never communicated with them, they were caring people. Do you think that what they took a little extra trouble to do was a good lesson for their children? And don't you think they felt good about it?

The second family retained cremation but with a simple private service. By far the biggest factor in increasing funeral costs is the desire to have the casket present in the funeral home for viewing or during a service. This will incur increases in the funeral director's services and the cost of a better quality casket. In addition, embalming may be required if the casket is to be opened to the public or if it remains unburied or uncremated for a period of time. There will be facility costs and the service charges will increase. The family will probably want a more presentable casket than the immediate cremation container, or the funeral director may not allow that container to be viewed by the public if it does not have an interior fabric lining. But the family has modified a traditional funeral to suit their needs and that has substantially reduced the cost they incur.

The first family is the type of client funeral directors love. They retain the old religious values and customs. They are likely to be sentimental and they will do things as their fathers and mothers did. They are also likely to seek the services of the funeral director who served their family in the past. They will buy expensive merchandise, often on the advice of the funeral director, and few could talk them out of spending the money. To them a funeral is a sign of honor and respect. They feel a bond of trust with the funeral director and they expect him to cater to their needs. Such an arrangement is fine with me so long as the family does not get cheated and receives everything it pays for.

In the mid-1980s, I realized that consumers were not aware of the alternative of immediate cremation. Funeral directors were not advertising it, and when they did the price it was generally offered at was far too high.

Recognizing a market, I proceeded to advertise in the telephone yellow pages in every directory for north and central New Jersey. My bill for that advertising was over $2,000 a month and I was locked in for a year. I priced the total immediate cremation funeral, which I advertised, at under $400. I reasoned that anyone seeking an inexpensive disposition would look in the yellow pages under the only suitable heading, "Funeral Directors" or "Cremation." My logo featured a lighthouse and in the beam of light was the name of the cremation service. When I sold my businesses three years later, that little sideline was doing very well.

All the competing local funeral directors in each directory had to do was undercut my price in their ads. Had they done so, I would have been out of the immediate cremation business in a year. That didn't happen and I made a nice profit. The funeral directors didn't want the immediate cremation work. What they wanted was the casket sale and full-service funeral. Times have changed. In 1993 in my area, ads for inexpensive cremations are plentiful.

7

The Funeral Arrangement Contract

Having read the previous chapter, you are aware of the many variations in services available to the funeral consumer. You also have some idea of what these services will cost. Here I will give you all the information you need to know about pricing. Chapter 8 will take you through the actual arrangement conference with the funeral director.

All funeral homes in the United States are governed by the Federal Trade Commission Rule. Copies of both the 1984 rule and the newly revised rule (effective July 19, 1994) can be found in the appendix of this book. The rule spells out what information must be provided to the consumer and in what form. It specifies how items are to be broken down on the arrangement contract and contains certain disclosure statements that the funeral director must make on that form.

The rule is designed to do two things: make it easier for the consumer to comparison shop funeral homes for price, and, having selected one, make funeral arrangements while being presented with nondeceptive pricing information. The information and prices, relevant to the family's decisions regarding the goods and services wanted, are transferred by the funeral director to the arrangement contract. That agreement is then signed by both parties and a copy is given to the consumer. It is now a binding contract of what the bereaved have purchased and attests that the funeral home is in compliance with the rule.

The rule governs not only the arrangement contract, but a General Price List and Outer Burial Container Price List. These items must be made available to a consumer who comes to the funeral home in person, and copies must be available for him to take. These lists must also be prominently displayed when arrangements are being made. This gives the consumer the opportunity to price shop in advance of the time of need.

Estimate # _____ Date _____   Funeral Service at _____
For the funeral of _____   Date _____ a.m. ____ p.m.
Address _____   Clergyman _____
_____   Address _____
Charge to _____   Organizational service by _____
_____   Date _____ a.m. ____ p.m.
_____ Tel. No. _____   Visiting _____

STATEMENT OF FUNERAL GOODS AND SERVICES SELECTED*

CATEGORY 1: PROFESSIONAL SERVICES

A. Arrangements and Supervision
  Funeral counseling, arranging, supervising, and conducting funeral; effecting interment, cremation, or transfer, records procuring, processing, and filing. All necessary correspondence and telephone communication; receiving and arranging floral tributes; staff assistance .... $_____
  Non-local interment .... $_____
  Non-local obtaining of death cert. .... $_____
  Non-salaries assistants .... $_____
  Other .... $_____
B. Preparation and Care of Deceased
  1. Embalming
    a. unautopsied .... $_____
    b. autopsied .... $_____
  2. Sanitary care without embalming .... $_____
  3. Dressing and casketing .... $_____
  4. Cosmetic application .... $_____
  5. Other .... $_____
                                    CATEGORY 1—TOTAL $_____

CATEGORY 2: FACILITY CHARGE

A. Use of Funeral Home for Visitation and/or Ceremony,
   #_____ of Days and Total .... $_____
B. Facility Charge, excluding Visitation and/or Ceremony .... $_____
C. Preparation Room .... $_____
D. Other .... $_____
                                    CATEGORY 2—TOTAL $_____

CATEGORY 3: TRANSPORTATION

A. Transfer of deceased to Funeral Home .... $_____
B. Use of Hearse .... $_____
C. Use of Limousine(s) .... $_____
D. Use of Flower car(s) .... $_____
E. Other .... $_____
                                    CATEGORY 3—TOTAL $_____

CATEGORY 4: MERCHANDISE

A. Casket (Description) _____
_____ $_____
B. Vault or Other Outer Enclosure (Description) _____
_____
C. Clothing .... $_____

*This form was developed by the author's funeral corporation. All "price range" information is based on "1990 Survey of Funeral Home Operators," National Funeral Directors Association (or, where noted, Mr. Young's experience).

D. Miscellaneous Items of Merchandise
    1. Register book .... $_____
    2. Prayer cards .... $_____
    3. Acknowledgment cards .... $_____
    4. Temporary Grave Marker .... $_____
E. Cremation Urn .... $_____
F. Other .... $_____

CATEGORY 4   TOTAL $_____

TOTAL OF FUNERAL CHARGES CATEGORIES 1–4 $_____

CATEGORY 5: CASH DISBURSEMENTS

Cemetery ....
.... opening ....
.... purchase ....
.... $_____
Cremation charge .... $_____
Disposition of Cremains .... $_____
Newspaper Notices ....
....
....
Death Certificates .... $_____
Burial/Cremation Permit .... $_____
................Pallbearers @ .... $ .... $_____
Gratuities .... $_____
Clergy honorarium .... $_____
Mass offering .... $_____
Organist .... $_____
Soloist .... $_____
Music .... $_____
Travel Tolls .... $_____
Telephone/Telegraph .... $_____
Air transportation charges .... $_____
Shipping charges .... $_____
Hairdressing .... $_____
Other _____
_____ $_____

CASH DISBURSEMENTS SUB-TOTAL CATEGORY 5 $_____
TOTAL OF FUNERAL CHARGES CATEGORIES 1-4 $_____
GRAND TOTAL $_____

Charges are only for those items that are used. If we are required by law to use any items, we will explain in writing.

If you selected a funeral which required embalming, such as a funeral with viewing, you may have to pay for embalming. You do not have to pay for embalming you did not approve if you selected arrangements such as a direct cremation or immediate burial. If we charged for embalming, we will explain why.

I have read and received the above itemization of Funeral Expenses:

_____
Signature of Person Making Arrangements

_____
Relationship to Deceased

_____
                                                 date

I have prepared the above itemization of Funeral Expenses:

_____
Signature of Practitioner   License #

Funeral directors are also required to give pricing information over the phone. A word of caution to the consumer: I would never answer the question "What does a funeral cost?" when asked over the phone. The sample arrangement contract form on pages 52 and 53 of this volume has approximately fifty price blanks that can be filled in. A funeral director cannot answer such a vague question and hope to be accurate. He can tell consumers the total for an immediate cremation. He can also give the cost of each component item. But until the funeral director actually makes a complete arrangement for a funeral, he cannot include every necessary item and give an accurate price. If a potential client were to receive an answer to the question "What does a funeral cost?" any quoted figure would probably be a "low ball" to get the family in his door.

Now let's look at each category on the sample arrangement contract form. The services or merchandise are broken down and explained, and finally, a price range is given. The average prices are taken from the "1990 Survey of Funeral Home Operations" conducted by the National Funeral Directors Association, Milwaukee, Wisconsin. The regions of the country, ranked from most expensive to least, are as follows: most expensive: 1. New England, 2. Middle Atlantic, 3. East North Central, 4. West North Central, 5. East South Central, 6. Pacific, 7. South Atlantic, 8. West South Central, and least expensive: 9. Mountain.

ARRANGEMENTS AND SUPERVISION

No matter how many synonyms we create "arrangements and supervision" is the funeral home's charge for the professional staff overhead. This figure never declines: when families make arrangements for a funeral, they automatically incur this charge. For a description of what the funeral director does to earn this money, see chapters 3 and 4. Because it does not decline there is no leeway for the consumer to save money here, with two exceptions: immediate cremation and immediate burial. Both require less professional supervision, i.e., less charges. There are provisions for additional charges to be tacked on for nonlocal necessities. If families are traveling to a cemetery outside the local area, they will be charged more because the funeral director has to take them there and see to the interment. The same is true if he chases down a death certificate or hires additional men not on the payroll. (Price range = $600 to $780)

PREPARATION AND CARE OF DECEDENT

Note that there are two types of embalming, "unautopsied" and "autopsied." Modern embalming consists of using the circulatory system of the body to inject chemicals that retard decomposition, increase sanitation, and provide cosmetic benefits. The solution is injected through an opening made in an artery and the blood it replaces is drained from a vein. The solution consists of a formaldehyde base with various additives to help the cosmetic results. A small surgical incision is made at what a layman would call a "pressure point," where the vessels are near the surface of the skin. The body cavity is treated by inserting a surgical tube known as a "trocar" through the abdomen so that the solution can saturate the cavity and the organs it contains. All this is true for an unautopsied body. An autopsied body has most likely had the body cavity and/or the head surgically examined by a pathologist. An autopsy requires more work, time, and chemicals for a funeral director, hence a higher charge. (Price range = $181 to $650*)

Sanitary care without embalming is exactly that: sometimes the body is surface disinfected. (Some states do have regulations requiring the embalming of a body that is out of refrigeration for a specific period of time.) This charge is minimal, no standard set, but I would guess $50.

"Other" refers to restorative art or the reconstruction of facial features out of necessity. This could be required for an accident victim whom the family wishes to view. The reconstruction is done by the funeral director first using surgical suturing techniques, then an embalmers wax to rebuild features. The results can be amazing if done by a talented funeral director. (Price range = an hourly rate of from $75 to $200)

"Dressing and Casketing" means the preparation after embalming to casket the deceased for viewing or for a service. The funeral director can supply clothing, but generally the clothing is more expensive than what a family can provide. The cost of the clothing can be found under "merchandise." Cosmetic application is necessary for an open casket if the deceased's appearance is important. (Price range = $57 to $125)

---

*This range takes into account special situations such as infectious disease or AIDS. The mid-range of $400 is close to standard.

USE OF FACILITIES

This charge is itemized to reflect the actual use of the funeral home. A room is set aside for each family having calling hours. The service can be held in that room or in a chapel set aside just for the service. Charges are based on the length of time the family occupies the room: a one-day viewing instead of two would incur less charge. There is a recent trend toward shorter viewing periods (Price range = $160 to $450 for one day of viewing or service). A viewing period of two hours in the afternoon and another two hours in the evening would be considered one day.

The "preparation room" is on overhead charge for where the embalming takes place. (Price range = roughly $100)

TRANSPORTATION

Of these potential charges, the first two are non-negotiable. For any handling of the deceased to take place, the body must be transported to the funeral home. Even if there are no services at the funeral home—for instance, in the case of immediate cremation—the deceased must still be transported to the place of burial or cremation. One word of caution: A hearse is a specially constructed car designed to hold a single casket. If your funeral arrangements state that you are paying for a hearse, *make sure you get one.* Vans or station wagons used to take cremation containers in multiples to a crematory are not hearses. Limousines are used to transport a family to the funeral home, the church, or the cemetery. They do provide a convenience to families who do not want to drive or who don't have their own vehicles. This item is an obvious place to cut expenses. In arranging for a funeral with cost in mind, paying for a limousine that is not truly needed can be an unwanted expense. Flower cars are used to take the floral arrangements that were with the casket at the funeral home to the place of interment or cremation. Often the consumer cannot decline a vehicle for this purpose, since funeral homes must dispose of the flowers and their containers somehow, and environmental laws and the cost of trash collection can make that difficult. Some churches or nursing homes will take the flowers. (I know of a nursing home that used them for classes in flower arranging.) An obvious solution is to ask for donations to a charity in lieu of flowers, or the family can take the flower arrangements after the services. These are a few ways to cut expenses. The line marked "other" on the funeral arrangement contract can refer to a car for the clergy or to pick up a relative. It need not be a limousine.

Price Ranges

Transfer to funeral home	= $75 to $120
Limousine	= $60 to $160
Flower car	= $50 to $150
Other	= $50 to $150

These charges are for local trips, usually under twenty-five miles. There are also charges based on mileage for longer trips. Having the interment a significant distance from the funeral home can cost more than the purchase of a new grave locally.

MERCHANDISE

The Casket

Once the consumer has decided on the type of funeral, the casket is the one single item that most directly affects the cost of the total funeral. If cremation without viewing has been chosen, it follows that the least expensive container for the deceased is probably desirable. If a funeral with a casket present has been chosen then the quality of the casket may be limited by religious considerations. But, if the consumer has a reason to choose a casket deemed suitable for viewing and he is not constrained by anything other than his own pocketbook, there are many to choose from.

Chapter 6 can help you decide on the type of service appropriate to your needs. This chapter tells you how to deal with the funeral director in selecting the casket, and will acquaint you with the merchandise currently available. Prices are broken down in two ways: How much it costs the funeral director to *buy* the *minimum* model of a specific type of casket, and what the cost is to the consumer for the *average* of that type.

Caskets are of four basic types: *wood, metal, sealed metal,* and *fiber glass.* Funeral directors will generally mark up (increase) the price of caskets from one to three times what they actually pay for them. A casket with a retail price of $750 was most likely sold to the funeral director for $200 to $300. *The single most important point to remember* *is that the funeral director can offer you a casket with an interior, suitable for viewing, for under $500 and still be making his normal profit.* The funeral director is not required to make available a minimum (economy model) casket at a set low price. If you are shown a minimum-priced casket, you may not like that choice for aesthetic reasons, but if you are not offered the minimum available when you are given the casket price list or shown into the casket display room, ask why the minimum-priced casket has not been made available to you. Funeral directors are not obligated to show consumers a minimum-priced casket, but if it is known that such a casket is available—as I am now making clear—then consumers can ask about this casket if it is something they want to consider. This is not a cadillac showroom, this is a "dealership" that should offer a balanced line of merchandise, both *inexpensive* and *expensive*. Caskets will either be "full open" or "half open." Whether the consumer chooses to have the whole body displayed or just the upper half depends on custom.

Wooden Caskets

Wooden caskets include pressed board covered on the exterior with a fabric commonly known in the trade as "grey cloth." That particular kind of casket, as well as the least expensive orthodox Jewish caskets, make up the bottom end of the price range for caskets suitable to be viewed. Orthodox caskets have no metal, such as hinges or handles, and no upholstered interior. If the wood is finished at all, it is a minimal color stain as opposed to a glossy finish. A casket's cost is determined by the quality of the finished wood and the quality of the interior fabric. If the deceased is going to have an open casket, there is generally an interior that resembles a bed with a pillow. The least expensive fabric is a shiny satin or rayon, usually in "eggshell" or off-white color. The mattress is the least expensive material available, often stuffed with processed wood shavings. The cost of the fabric increases as the quality moves up from rayon to velvet. Velvet is stitched in a variety of decorative ways. A recent trend has been to have the open casket lid adorned with a design or scene, visible when the deceased is being viewed. Trees seem to be a popular decorative item. This least expensive casket is available to the funeral director for about $160.

Metal Caskets

The next rung on the casket price ladder is occupied by "nonprotective" metal. Such caskets are usually made of 20-gauge steel which has been welded. They generally have clips that hold the top down and have no type of gasket or protective locking devices. This type of casket is available in any color the manufacturer can spray paint. The cost is determined by how fancy the finish, handles, and interior are. As interior fabrics get softer in texture, have better stitching, and nicer colors, the cost goes up. As the handles get more expensive and corner decoration is screwed on, the price goes up. Why would a special color interior be wanted? The color of the clothing the deceased will wear plays a part in this decision. Why do cars come in so many colors? Personal taste! The funeral director can buy this type of casket for about $250. The average cost to the consumer is $750.

We now move on to the "sealed" metal caskets. What is added to the "nonsealers" is a rubber gasket and more substantial latching devices. Some have latches at the end which consist of a long threaded rod that, when cranked, pulls pins down into the gasket. A cap is then placed over the opening where the crank was inserted. The least expensive of this type has a simple lever-lock visible on the front of the casket. The gauge of metal will get thicker as the cost goes up: 16-gauge steel is thicker and more costly than 20-gauge steel. Most minimum "sealers" are the same gauge steel and the same casket shells as the "nonsealers." Add a rubber gasket where the lid meets the lower part, latches instead of clips, and you have a "sealer." The cost to the funeral director has jumped to about $300 for the minimum sealer. Notice that by paying $50 more than a nonsealer costs, he sells it to you and makes and additional $100 to $150 when the mark-up is figured in. Sealed caskets make the consumer consider crossing the line from choosing a casket that is merely aesthetically pleasing, to entertaining the possibility that protecting the body from the elements is important. That is a very personal decision. Some above-ground mausoleums require sealed caskets or a soldered-closed metal box before the deceased can be placed in the crypt. The only times that a sealed metal casket might be required are: the occasional shipping situation in which the casket is transported on a common ground, sea, or air carrier (but this need for a sealed casket is rarely the case when the deceased is being transported within the United States); or if the deceased is badly decomposed and cannot be embalmed. The funeral director may make this a requirement in such cases, or the state law may mandate it.

Warranties! The smart funeral director has a phrase on the arrangement contract form that says he makes no representations about warranties. What comes from the manufacturer is what you get. Read it carefully. I have never seen a manufacturer's warranty that didn't say something to the affect of, "Will replace if found to be defective." Under what scenario are you going to remove someone from the grave to see if the sealed metal casket performed properly? Maybe this will occur if you are moving a family plot to another location, or if the interment was above ground and the end plate of the mausoleum space was removed for some reason. Sealed metal caskets serve as marketing tools for the funeral director. If the consumer thinks the sealing is an advantage, then the purchase of this type of casket should be considered. The funeral director can buy the minimum model of sealed metal casket for about $300, but because he wants a bigger spread in price between the inexpensive nonsealer and more expensive sealer, he will upgrade the latter's interior, sometimes to velvet, and the cost jumps. At this level the manufacturer has also added an adjustable spring bed mattress. This may sound silly, but it does help the funeral director to position the body. The adjustable mattress allows the body to be raised, lowered, or tilted to one side. When a body is displayed, it is generally raised in the casket and slightly tilted toward the person viewing the deceased. (Average cost to the consumer = $1,770)

Grouped in this same price range are solid wood caskets. Once the standard and available at reasonable cost, today solid wood caskets cannot be as easily produced as welded steel ones. They are more labor intensive and designed to let the beauty of the various woods show through the finish. The cost for such fine caskets varies with the type of wood. On a scale of least expensive to most expensive we find: poplar, pine, birch, oak, cherry, mahogany, and walnut. In the lower-cost ranges other regional softwoods may be used. The consumer may want to consider this type because of the aesthetic value of the wood. The analogy to purchasing furniture is the closest I can come to giving a reason why one type of wood is preferred over another. I have often heard that comment made by consumers while in the casket showroom. The cost to the funeral director would be about $650, while the average cost to the consumer is $1,700.

We now move into exotic territory. Caskets can be had that are made of stainless steel, copper, or bronze. The very best are not welded, but are bronze and have been cast in one piece. Cast bronze is measured in ounces, not by gauge, with 32 ounces being standard, 48 ounces an option. The cost to the funeral director can be as high as $5,000, but on the average the consumer buys noncast caskets of copper and stainless steel for just over $3,000.

Fiber Glass Caskets

There has been no discussion of fiber glass caskets. Fiber glass is derived from a mold and does not require any type of work to obtain a finish on the exterior, as is the case with wood or metal. At this point in time they are a rarity. Several years ago there was an attempt by an independent distributor to set up retail distribution direct to the consumer. To my knowledge these efforts were not successful. It is not difficult to understand why the public has not flocked to fiber glass as a casket material. The ones currently available are more expensive than welded steel. Perhaps the market for them will grow, but the funeral industry is rooted in tradition and change comes slowly. Finally, why choose one type of casket over another? It was my practice to have any merchandise arranged by price. I gave the funeral purchaser the total cost of all goods and services, including cash disbursements to other providers (such as the cemetery), before showing any caskets. I said, and all funeral directors who worked for me were instructed to say, "This is your total cost. The only additional expense is the casket. The caskets are arranged by price. I will show you the least expensive one first and then illustrate the features that result in higher-priced caskets."

At this point the funeral consumer was taken into the casket display room. In a few minutes' time the different finishes and interiors were pointed out. The locking devices were then shown as well as the sealed and metal caskets. Finally, the client was told, "Selecting a casket should be based on personal taste. I cannot tell you what features are important to you, or how much you should spend. I will leave you to make a selection. If you have a question, I will be in the room where we made the arrangements." Then I left the room. Section 6 (e) (1) of the Federal Trade Commission Rule states that it is deceptive to "represent that funeral goods or services will delay the natural decomposition of human remains for the long term or an indefinite time." That notwithstanding, many people select a sealed casket. It is all personal taste.

Two final words on caskets: It is not unusual for a funeral director to reduce the amount of markup on his high-end merchandise since he can obtain the same profit from a smaller markup on expensive items. Finally, "minimum alternative containers," which the consumer generally does not see—those suitable for cremation—are available in cardboard, composite board, or inexpensive planks. They wholesale for under $25 in cardboard, more in other materials. The average cost to the consumer is $132.

BURIAL VAULTS (OUTER BURIAL CONTAINERS)

Concrete and steel are the two types of available vaults. The selection is much more limited than with caskets. Concrete is the most common type because steel isn't used in all areas of the country. A vault is placed in the grave and serves as a container for the casket. The practical application for the cemetery is that it keeps the ground from collapsing in the case of plots designed to accommodate more than one burial. For that reason, some cemeteries require their use. The practical application for the consumer is that if a grave is opened "double depth" or "triple depth" and a vault is placed on the bottom, another vault may be placed on top, thus putting more than one casket in a vertical grave opening.

Steel vaults can be either galvanized or nongalvanized and are made of either 10-gauge or 12-gauge steel. Sometimes referred to as "bell type," they have a platform on which the casket is placed, then the one-piece rectangular top is lowered over the casket onto the base. To test how the concept of a vault works, simply use the old science trick of placing an empty glass, opening down, into water. The water can only rise so far before the trapped air keeps it from rising any further. Steel vaults can also be configured like concrete vaults, a rectangle with a lid that fits on, but this is not common. The cost to the consumer for a nongalvanized steel vault averages about $784; galvanized steel vaults cost about $1,090.

Concrete vaults come in these configurations:

Unfinished concrete with a heavy lid that is not sealed, but simply placed on (average cost to the consumer is $403).

Asphalt-coated concrete with a heavy lid that is held on by tongue and groove, and sealed (average cost to the consumer is $571).

Asphalt-coated concrete with an inner lining, nonmetallic (average cost to the consumer is $692).

Asphalt-coated concrete with stainless steel or copper lining (average cost to the consumer is $1,500 and up [estimated]).

CLOTHING

The funeral director keeps clothing for both men and women in stock, including outer garments and undergarments. Recently there has been a trend to get away from the formality of dress long associated with funerals. (Black was the choice of suit color.) Today, the casketed person is more likely to wear what the family regards as his or her normal attire. The first choice of family members is to bring clothing from home. This is particularly true if the deceased is a younger person. Consumers should try to use what they are familiar with. If clothing needs to be purchased, check retail stores for cost. Often they can be less expensive and the selection is probably better.

REGISTER BOOK

It is normal to have one of these books available for visitors to sign as they enter to view the body or attend a service. It can be at the funeral home for visiting hours, at the church for the service, or at home if a Jewish family sits Shiva and receives visitors there. This book generally contains the name of the deceased and the relatives. Such books can be quite ornate and designed for a specific religious or ethnic group. (Average cost to the consumer = $20)

PRAYER CARDS

Used primarily by those of the Catholic faith, they can be used for Protestant services as well. They are printed cards with an appropriate prayer along with the name and dates of birth and death of the deceased. Some people keep them as mementos and they are usually displayed with the register book and available for visitors to pick up. They usually come in a box of 100. (Average cost to the consumer = $35)

ACKNOWLEDGMENT CARDS

These are "Thank Yous" for people who have sent flowers, donations, or in some way caused the family of the deceased to wish to acknowledge their participation in the funeral. (Average cost to the consumer = $20)

TEMPORARY GRAVE MARKER

It normally takes some time for a stone to be made to mark a grave. If a stone is already present (as is the case, for example, when one spouse precedes the other in death) and the name of the person just interred there can be added, there is little need for this temporary aluminum or plastic marker. (Average cost to the consumer = $20)

CREMATION URN

Cremated remains come from the crematory in temporary containers usually made of cardboard or plastic lined with a plastic bag. A cremation urn is a more suitable container for permanent storage. The urn can be interred in a family grave, displayed in a niche in a cemetery mausoleum, or retained by the family. They are made of wood, metal, or stone. Prices can vary dramatically from a minimum of $50 to as much as several hundred dollars.

OTHER

Funeral directors have other items available. Religious emblems for inside the casket, and name plates for the outside of the casket are just a couple.

CASH DISBURSEMENTS

These are goods and services for which the funeral director advances money for the convenience of the family. The funeral director may not mark up these items unless he tells the consumer. The Federal Trade Commission Rule expressly forbids this markup unless full disclosure has been given. Most funeral directors require that this section of the arrangement contract be paid at the time of the funeral. What he is doing is acting as your agent and banker to see that these necessities are accomplished. He may ask that you make a check out directly to the cemetery or to the clergy.

CEMETERY

Chapter 5 deals extensively with the cemetery. Readers are encouraged to review that chapter. Cemetery charges vary widely depending on numerous factors, and the space on the arrangement form is for the funeral director to fill in once he has explored with the consumer all the available possibilities. *Discuss the cemetery options fully with the funeral director.* Remember that he does not make money on the cemetery charges. He does, however, want to sell merchandise. Questions should begin to occur to the consumer: Is there a cemetery that does not require a vault? Can I avoid hearse and limousine charges by going to a local cemetery? If a specific mausoleum requires a sealed metal casket, do I really want a space there? Most families with roots in a particular area of the country will want to have the most recent death in the family returned to them for burial. They will absorb the costs to transport the remains. If the consumer does not own grave space already, it is helpful to know *all* the cemetery charges and requirements before investing in a new plot.

CREMATION CHARGE

This is exactly what the crematory charges the funeral director for the act of cremating the deceased. It is a part of the quoted charges for a cremation, either immediate or with a service, and must be revealed within that total as a cash disbursement. It usually will be about $100 to $200 and in some states cremation may be allowed at the funeral home that handles all the arrangements. In other states it is done only in a cemetery. Disposition of cremated remains is discussed fully in chapter 5.

NEWSPAPER NOTICES

There are two types of notices, "Obituaries" and "Paid Death Notices." Each newspaper has its own format. Some papers consider obituaries to be news and are very happy to print them, along with service times, free of charge. They are informative paragraphs written as a story about a person's life. Paid death notices are more formal, concentrate on survivors and service times, and are not news items. Such notices are generally charged to the funeral home by the paper. They are based on length, and, again, the funeral director can only pass the charge on to the consumer.

THE DEATH CERTIFICATE

The death certificate is the legal record of a person's death. The funeral director will obtain, from the person authorizing the services, specific statistical information regarding the deceased. Usually it is a variation on the following: full legal name, mother's and father's names, date of birth, legal address, place of birth, employment, Social Security number, veteran status, marital status, next of kin. The person who pronounces the individual dead fills in a section of medical history and the cause of death, as well as the time and place of death. The funeral director fills in the place of burial and his license number. The finished certificate is filed permanently with the proper government authority, usually a municipal registrar of vital statistics. A charge is made by that authority for copies which are used for legal purposes such as collecting life insurance, veteran's benefits, Social Security death benefit, transferring car titles and mortgages, probating a will, and the like. They usually come with a raised seal indicating that they are originals. Some agencies will accept a certificate in photocopy form if the seal is visible. (Average cost to the consumer = $3 to $5 per copy)

THE BURIAL/CREMATION PERMIT

This form is necessary in order to cremate or bury the deceased and is issued by the authority that records the death certificate. (Average cost to the consumer = $1 to $3)

PALLBEARERS

These are the persons designated to carry the casket from the funeral home to the hearse and from the hearse to the service (if it's in a church) or to the grave site. Hired by the funeral director, the number varies according to the need. A funeral going into church will need them, or perhaps they will be needed at the cemetery. The consumer can avoid this charge by supplying his own. Often, the funeral director can tip a driver of a limousine, or other available help, and avoid hiring staff just to be pallbearers. This can also be an honorary position occupied by family or friends where no actual carrying is done. (Average cost to the consumer is $25 per person)

GRATUITIES

Tips can be given to cemetery help to carry a casket, or to the vault installers. If it saves the consumer additional charges, pay it. If it is money given to morgue attendants, security guards, and the like to help the funeral director do his job more easily, the funeral director should absorb the cost.

CLERGY HONORARIUM/MASS OFFERING

As a general rule, if the family does not have a relationship with a member of the clergy and asks the funeral director to obtain one for a service, that service must be paid for. Mass fees are charged by churches to the consumer to have the service conducted in the church. The costs can vary considerably, particularly between urban areas and small towns. (Average cost to the consumer = $50 to $200)

ORGANIST/SOLOIST/MUSIC

Most funeral homes are equipped to play music on tape. If a request is made for individuals to perform, they will charge. Some churches include this fee in their mass offering, some do not. Some will allow the option of an organist without a soloist. Each situation can be different. What the consumer wishes is a matter of personal taste. (Average cost to the consumer = $25 to $50 per performer)

TRAVEL

The group of charges relating to "travel" can be incurred if the deceased is transported over a distance. The major charge can apply when a death occurs away from where the services will be held. *If death occurs out of state, call the funeral director where the services and burial will be held. Let him hire the shipping funeral director.* All funeral directors have "shipping firms" they deal with. The firm doing the shipping acts as the subcontractor for the funeral home the consumer has hired. Your local funeral director knows how to control the shipping costs to benefit his client. There are many horror stories of people who suffered the death of a loved one away from home and were charged exorbitant amounts by funeral directors who performed the shipping. The funeral director at home knows how to control these charges, i.e., what is necessary and what is not. He will also take the burden off of the consumer at an emotional time when his client may be thinking less rationally. It is to his benefit to keep as much of the charges at the receiving end as he possibly can. (Average cost to the consumer = $450 to $750, plus air fare or motor vehicle transportation)

HAIRDRESSING

This seems rather obvious, but often a funeral director will routinely include the charge in his own preparation fees if someone on staff is capable of doing the work. If a hairdresser is called in, there can be a separate charge.

OTHER

This covers any additional cash disbursement to a third party that the funeral director has not anticipated. A good example may be an escort to the cemetery for an extremely large funeral procession,* or hiring a local funeral director to meet the funeral at an out-of-state cemetery.

A thorough reading of this chapter should make it difficult for consumers to be sold goods and services not wanted. If you want to use this information to its fullest, and you have time to do so, obtain sample price lists from several funeral homes in your area. Put their list next to these explanations and decide what services you do and do not need.

---

*In some localities this escort is provided by the police as a public service. Check with your local police department.

8

The Funeral Arrangement Conference: Selecting a Funeral Director

If your family does not have a funeral director when a death occurs, a selection has to be made. If the death occurs away from home, a decision has to be made as to where the funeral service will be held. First, if all the funeral director in the out-of-town location is doing is shipping the deceased to your funeral director at home, *let the funeral director at home contract for the other services.* Remember, knowledge is the consumer's weapon in holding down costs. For instance, he can prevent you from buying an expensive casket for shipment of the body. A heavier casket increases the transportation charges that the airlines assess. Consumers are also susceptible to being sold an inferior casket at a high price if they are out-of-town and the distant funeral director is not likely to see them again. Your home funeral director does not want you to spend money with another funeral director. He will know who to hire at the most reasonable rate in the area where the death occurred. He can easily look up firms that specialize in preparation and shipping. I can relate numerous horror stories about people who arrived at my funeral home to make arrangements for the services after having the deceased shipped to us. Think back to the woman on page 36 whose husband died out of state; she was handed a phone book open to the yellow pages. She was sold clothing, an expensive casket, and paid preparation charges that were too high; she was then told that my charges were going to be minimal.

She was shocked to find that the cemetery charges were higher than she had been told the *whole* funeral would be. Had she called me first, I would have hired a firm in that area specializing in shipping at about one-tenth of what she paid. She also would have been spared the trauma of the business dealings she was unprepared for. We would simply have asked her, "Do you want us to arrange to have him shipped to us by the least expensive means?" and hired the other funeral director.

If you have never hired a funeral director in your area, and need one, previous contact is your best barometer for choosing one. Have you been to a funeral in any of the funeral homes available to you? Were you greeted when you entered by a competent person who made you feel at home, or did you wander into a hall with signs indicating which family was where and left to find your own way? Did the family you went there to visit express an opinion on the service they received? If you knew them well enough to visit for their funeral, don't you know them well enough to ask them how that funeral home treated them?

Funeral directors with affiliations in the community expect to have recommendations given by people you probably know. Clergy are a prime source. They have had a chance to deal with the funeral directors on a business basis and respect some more than others.

If you have no way of establishing a personal contact, you are now in the unenviable position of having to shop. It is unlikely you do not know at least a name or two. Funeral directors spend a great deal of money to get their names out. You can find their ads on bingo cards, bus stop booths, every athletic program and social event program in existence, church calendars, bridge club tallies, and billboards. Funeral directors are the mainstays of service clubs and fraternal organizations.

If you have been reading the obituaries in the newspaper and one funeral home gets the lion's share, there is probably a good reason. If there is no other way to make a selection, go to the telephone directory yellow pages. The ads will tell you a lot about who placed them. What do they stress in their ads? Most will stress a tradition of trust based on years of service. Is the name of the manager the same as the name of the funeral home? If not, the owner probably bought his "tradition" when he purchased an old family funeral home from the original owners. There may be very substantive information indicating a willingness to give low-cost pricing. Advertising "cremation" is a sure sign that the funeral home has no trouble breaking from the traditional funeral and its costs.

When you call, ask for financial data on the phone. They should have no problem quoting a price for immediate cremation. If you want to really put them to the test, ask them the cost of the minimum casket on display in their showroom. If they play dodge ball, call someone else. In fairness, be aware that they cannot give "unit prices." That is a fancy way of saying they cannot give you a straight answer if you ask, "How much is a funeral with two days visiting?" You won't get an accurate answer, because there are so many items that need to be determined before an exact price can be given. That is why I recommend asking for the price of the least expensive casket they display. We are looking for a willingness to provide inexpensive alternatives as an indication of whose needs the funeral director is really trying to satisfy.

When you make that initial call to arrange a funeral conference, pay attention to who answers the phone. Is it a secretary who tells you she sets up appointments, takes down the information, and then schedules you for 10:00 to meet with a funeral director? Or does she say, "Please hold for a moment so I can put Mr. Jones, one of our funeral directors, on the phone with you." They can be a large funeral home, but still maintain customer focus. Do they ask you what your needs are, or do they begin by telling you that when you come in you should bring the following items? A desire to meet your needs means they will ask you what type of service you want. I usually asked, "Are you considering a funeral service in either the funeral home or a church?" The answer I received then allowed me to start planning for a full-service funeral. Since I was familiar with all the churches and clergy in the area, I knew what questions had to be asked of the family making the arrangements once they gave me that one answer. Remember the three conditions that must exist for the funeral director to properly act as your agent? Condition number 2 was the funeral director's ability to properly elicit from you what your desires are. If you don't like what you hear at that initial contact, thank him and go somewhere else. Your comfort level should come first.

THE CONSUMER'S BEST PROTECTION
Be Ready to Ask Questions!

I never worried about what time of the day or night people called me. For twenty years I was instantly awake when the phone rang and the habit won't go away. It was not unusual for me to take down detailed information from a person at 3:00 A.M., go back to sleep, and wake up at 7:00 A.M. to see if I had dreamed the conversation. On the other hand, I was always prepared to get dressed and head for the funeral home, meet an assistant, and go to work. I lived with "beepers" and cellular phones twenty-four hours a day. Even when I could well afford to delegate the responsibility for the initial phone contact to my staff or to an answering service, I tried hard not to do so.

When a death has occurred, the family of the deceased would prefer not to talk to a stranger about the arrangements. They want the confidence of knowing that their problems are understood by someone they can relate to, a person who can reinforce that they are doing the right thing. My experience is that even the most educated or accomplished business person rarely knows what questions to ask. People expect to be led through the decision-making process once they have expressed their basic needs. The funeral director who is responding to a family for the second, or third, or tenth time has a tremendous advantage. He can look into past records for grave information, relative's names, and merchandise sold. That familiarity must be treated as a trust. Remember my description of the community funeral homes and the ethnic and religious communities they serve. *A consumer's worst enemy can be the comfort of dealing with a funeral director he trusts just because he has the same religious or ethnic heritage.* It is not unlike the car salesman your family always used who slides you into the seat of a car he cannot sell and tells you it is the best buy on the lot. Do you know the difference? *Do not be afraid to ask about alternatives to the way things have always been!* Just because your aunt had three days of visiting for your uncle does not mean that the same visiting hours are appropriate or desirable for your father or mother. That casket you buried mom in has gone up 300 percent since her funeral. Do you really want that same casket for your dad, or would you rather have me tell you I can get one that looks almost identical for the same price you paid for your mom's?

YOUR FIRST CALL TO THE FUNERAL DIRECTOR

Presumably you now know what funeral director you want to call at the time of need. Upon placing the call you can expect to be asked the following questions:

1. Who has died?

2. Where is that person now?

3. Who pronounced the person dead and who is the attending physician?

4. Who is the next of kin?

5. Will that person (in #4) be making the arrangements?

6. Can you give me an idea as to what type of arrangements you want? Will there be a funeral in the funeral home or at a church? Where will the burial be?

7. When would you like to come in to make arrangements? (Or, more likely: Can you come in tomorrow at 9:00 A.M.?)

The funeral director has calculated several things while talking to you. He has a general idea of the services he must perform, and he is already weighing his needs for staff and facilities to accomplish your requests. He may choose to remove the person immediately from where death occurred, or he may wait, depending on his staff needs and whether or not embalming is necessary. For instance, a body may have to be embalmed or buried within a certain period of time because of state law or as a result of some religious requirement. If he removes it from refrigeration at the hospital, he is committed to a time schedule. If he leaves it there, he has options. He may put off the making of the arrangements until the afternoon because his staff is fully committed to other funerals. Conversely, he may try to get you right in because the day is going to get increasingly busy. I could easily put people off by saying, "I want to take care of you myself and I am tied up until 4:00 P.M. Tell your friends that having visiting hours tomorrow is all right. Put together the newspaper information; we have plenty of time to make their deadline. In the meantime, I will see to it that your father is removed from the hospital and prepared." I never used the word "embalmed" during the initial phone contact until the state told me I had to (I thought the term was too crass). In some places a permission slip must be signed by the family prior to embalming taking place.

If the family can make two decisions before arriving at the funeral home, the rest of the arrangements will fall into place. These two decisions will allow the funeral director to present the rest of the alternatives available:

1. What are the basic components of the actual funeral ceremony and where will it be held? Will there be a religious ceremony and, if so, will it be held at the funeral home, in a place of worship, or at the place of interment?

2. Where will the actual interment take place, and will it be burial (in whatever form that might take) or cremation?

Every other decision is triggered by these two initial ones. Once the funeral director knows that your loved one was a member of a specific church or temple and that the service is being held there, he knows what that particular clergy or group requires. When he knows where the place of interment is, he knows what the cemetery charges are for each specific aspect of the burial. He will know, for example, that one cemetery requires that it be notified forty-eight hours ahead of time in order to open a grave, while another requires less notice. One cemetery may require that a vault be used, while another does not. These are the areas of the funeral where the director, acting as your agent, can make the experience less frustrating by offering alternatives of which the consumer is not aware. Unlike the consumer, if the funeral director is not familiar with a specific church, temple, or cemetery, he knows what questions to ask. If he has been able to elicit this information from you before you arrive, he will be much better prepared and your arrangement conference will be far less of a strain.

THE ACTUAL CONFERENCE

You will want to arrive at the funeral home with all the papers necessary for supplying information. Though the *death certificate* is filed by the funeral director and contains vital statistic information about the person who has died as well as the medical information related to the death, the funeral director should tell you to come with the vital information he needs to execute the form. You should also write down the names of the survivors as you want them to appear in the newspaper notices. Also, if a plot or mausoleum is owned, try to locate any cemetery documents. Bring the clothing you want the deceased to wear and a recent picture if you are considering an open casket. If the deceased has false teeth, bring them. Consider using a woman's own makeup or wig (if the deceased wore one). The more help you can give the funeral director in making the person look as you knew him or her, the more pleased you will be.

Funeral directors have different styles in making arrangements. Some sit around a table with the family, while others prefer to be more formal and sit behind a desk. Perhaps a secretary may take the vital statistic information and then turn the family over to a funeral director. Most funeral homes prefer that the funeral director handle everything.

The opening conversation can be most difficult, particularly if the family and the funeral director do not know each other. I used the opening statements to introduce myself, then elicit information about the circumstances of the death. How the family responded, and who responded, gave me a lot of information about their emotional state. In talking about the circumstances of the death, people display emotion. If people are emotionally distraught, the task of decision-making can be difficult for them. On other occasions the death has been expected and there is a sense of relief in the room.

If the wife of the deceased is present and the conversation is dominated by one of the sons or daughters, I often turn the conversation directly to the widow to make sure the funeral is in accordance with her wishes. This may sound very humanitarian and considerate, and it is, but from a practical standpoint the next of kin must legally authorize the arrangements and is the one ultimately responsible for the bill (unless, of course, the will specifies that the next-of-kin is not to have that right). I remember one young man whose wife had just died, leaving him with two small children. He came to arrange the funeral, accompanied by his in-laws. The parents wanted two days of visiting, a flower car, and a limousine. In addition, grave space had to be purchased. The young man finally asked to see me outside. He told me he had no money. The parents lived down the street and I had known them for years. They said they would, "help out with the bill." They assured me they would come in the day after the funeral and pay me. I had the young man sign the arrangement form because legally he had to authorize the funeral. I then paid the church and cemetery out of my check book. Needless to say, at this point, twenty years later, I own the grave in which the young man's wife is buried. The parents showed up the day after the funeral, but they paid me only $75 for the limousine they rode in! The young man moved out of state shortly after. Of course I tried to collect the money. Ultimately I lost not only my profit, but the money I paid to purchase the casket and the vault she was buried in, the cash I put out for the church and pallbearers, and even the purchase of the grave. To this day the father says hello to me when we meet.

Today it would be difficult for a similar situation to happen. *Remember: what is being arranged is a legally binding contract.* Funeral directors have become better business persons as a result of Federal Trade Commission requirements. The FTC told us what the arrangement contract had to contain and we became acutely aware of the legalities. If that rule had been in effect when I was buying graves for people, no doubt the parents would have signed the form also! I always felt ill at ease in asking more than the next of kin to sign. I felt as though I was implicitly saying "I don't trust you." The FTC forced me to put the contract in front of people and present it as a straightforward business deal. It made my job much easier and improved my cash flow tremendously! The consumer can expect to make a down payment on the contract. This is generally a percentage of the total cost, or at least the estimated cash disbursements the funeral director must pay on the family's behalf.

The exercise of finding out who is really in charge and directing the conversation toward the next-of-kin when necessary is an attempt to give a family exactly what it needs. This is the time when families must think of the needs of the person closest to the deceased. It was not unusual for me to recognize spouses who were trying to communicate to the rest of the family that they did not want the type of service that was being forced upon them by their own families. Maybe these spouses lack the money the adult children think they have and the survivors can only spend half of what the children want to spend. On the other hand, maybe the children want to keep as much of the parents' money intact as they can, but the surviving spouse wants to spend it. Ultimately the funeral director must fall back on the rights of the next-of-kin and the assurance that he has enough security to collect on the funeral. A sure way to stop overzealous spenders is to inform them that they have to guarantee the cost of the funeral and be financially responsible.

Refer again to my three criteria to assure that you, as a consumer, are getting what you want. The first criterion: "Is the funeral director acting in your interest?" When I was in practice, I tried not to commit to promising a specific room for a family's use if I could avoid it. Why? Because I might be visited by another family needing a new set of funeral arrangements after I had completed a previous funeral. I wanted the flexibility to give the largest room to the family who needed it the most, and that might be the last family with whom I made arrangements. Maybe I needed to assure that the family leaving for church at 10:00 A.M. did not have to go past a room with a 10:00 A.M. funeral service in progress.

Be wary of statements like, "I wouldn't start visiting hours until the day after tomorrow. The newspaper notice won't appear until the morning and your friends might not see it in time." This is a valid point, but be prepared to ask if there is an extra facility charge for holding the body over. Is the funeral director really thinking that all his staff is committed to a morning funeral going out of town, and to be ready for your family he has to pay someone overtime or hire someone he can't charge you for? Whose convenience is being served? *Ask why the funeral director is recommending something if you do not understand or are uncomfortable with the recommendation.* Do not think that you are being disrespectful to the deceased by being practical regarding the arrangements. The funeral director's recommendation may very well save you time and money as well as being convenient. If he levels with you and tells you he has a business conflict, you can decide to either help him out or demand that you be accommodated. Perhaps you do not mind waiting the extra day for the room you want, provided you are not charged extra and he realizes the inconvenience you are willing to accept.

When the details of the arrangements are completed, you must do two things before selecting any merchandise:

1. Go over the contract form line by line and review the charges;

2. If the funeral director does not offer, *demand* that he tell you the exact total cost *before* you select any merchandise.

In addition to the specific services performed and rendered, you are about to make the decision that can most directly affect the cost of the funeral—the selection of the merchandise. Paying more than you want to for a casket and/or vault is not like buying a car you are unable to afford. Every time you start up that beauty in the garage there is a likelihood that you will get the same fuzzy feelings back that made you buy the car in the first place. But once the casket or vault is interred three days after you bought it, it is gone forever except in your memory. This is *not* the time for the consumer to be led by the funeral director. Now is the time for the consumer to do the leading. What the funeral director says before entering the selection room where the caskets are displayed is the biggest single indicator of just how well the consumer really is being treated.

In chapter 7, under the section dealing with the arrangement itemization, the various types of caskets, costs, markups, and features were discussed. Here we will deal with the display room and the selection process.

What the funeral director has just told you, in preparation for showing you the caskets, is designed to make the transition from the arrangement conference to the process of selecting merchandise. Most funeral directors today have that selection room on the premises, which is a big advantage to them in that they completely control what you see and how it is displayed. Refer to chapter 7 under "Caskets" and, upon your first glimpse at the casket room, look for the cloth-covered casket that should sell for around $450 to $500. If the funeral director has started the selection process by showing it to you first, chances are you are being treated fairly. If, on the other hand, the least expensive casket you can find is over $700, you are not being afforded a chance to pick the most economical casket available to be viewed. If that cloth-covered casket is priced at more than $525, it has been marked up more than is generally acceptable.

CONSUMER-CONSCIOUS FUNERAL DIRECTOR	PROFIT-DRIVEN FUNERAL DIRECTOR
There are three types of caskets: wood, metal, and sealed metal. Your selection is strictly a personal choice.	Your family has always used sealed metal. I doubt that you would want the others.
If you think protecting the body is important, perhaps you should consider a sealed metal casket. Otherwise, I would base my decision on how the casket looks.	What would your father think if he knew you were burying his wife in a casket that didn't seal?
At this point you have spent a total of $_____ and the only purchase left is the casket. Simply add the cost displayed on the casket to the total I gave you.	I'll add up the bill after you select a casket.
Our caskets are arranged by price with the least expensive first. After I show you where each type is, I will leave you alone to make your decision.	Let me show you the model that most of our clients choose.
The least expensive casket displayed is the most reasonable we can obtain.	Yes, I can find you a less expensive casket but most people don't use it.
Yes, the least expensive model I showed you is the most reasonable model available with an interior lining.	We keep our less expensive caskets in another room. If you really want to see them, I'll show them to you.

The key idea in this situation is to have the least expensive merchandise readily available for your consideration. If you do not see it, ask for it. If you get an evasive answer, you are being manipulated. How the caskets are merchandised is an entirely different matter. In my funeral homes I had them arranged by cost: the least expensive models were first to the customer's right as he entered. Of course, that cloth-covered casket was on the bottom of a two-tier rack, the only display in the room with one casket floor level and another directly over the top of it. Because of the configuration of the room, the most expensive hardwood ended up to be directly across from the least expensive. That is like putting a diamond chip next to the Hope diamond. The point is, however, that the least expensive casket was readily displayed and available, clients did not have to ask for it. Rarely did I sell it.

Another technique in discouraging a sale is to use an interior fabric not necessarily complementary to the casket. Fabric texture, color, and style can all be used to make an interior less attractive, as has been discussed. If you are shown a casket that is suitable, but has an interior not up to your standards, ask if it is available with a different interior.

When you have been shown the various types of caskets and their locations, you will want the opportunity to shop on your own. It is a very good idea to have someone with you who is as detached as possible from the emotional impact of what you are doing. You are going to be in the physical presence of the casket for only a very limited period of time. The only criteria for selecting a casket whose quality is above the necessary minimum are:

1. You don't like the appearance and would feel more comfortable with a better one.

2. You feel that "protection" for the deceased after interment is important to you.

3. You don't care what it costs; you have a need for a better-quality purchase.

If the consumer is accompanied by someone who can offer objective advice, that person should remind the purchaser of what his or her needs really are. After selecting the casket, the next concern will be a vault. The vault can be chosen beforehand, but I suggest the casket selection first.

The burial vault selection is more limited. The funeral director should have told you if a vault is required in the cemetery you are using. If it is not required, there are two considerations:

1. If I place it into the grave being used for this funeral, will it enable me to reopen the grave for another interment on top of it? In other words, is it more cost effective to buy a vault, bury this casket "double deep," and have additional use of the

vertical grave space; or is it less expensive to buy another grave next to this one for future use if need be?

2. Do I feel better knowing that the casket is in a burial vault?

The choices available when selecting vaults were described in chapter 7. After selecting a vault, you may want to select burial garments. Generally they are available from the funeral home at a more reasonable cost than if you were to buy something new in a store. This is particularly true of the mens' clothing, which is generally just a suit and tie. Women's clothing may be more expensive in a retail store, but the selection is much better there. Garments made for burial tend to be plain and of poor quality. In either case—whether the deceased is male or female—I recommend using the person's own clothing whenever possible.

At the conclusion of your selection, you will be taken back to the room where the arrangement conference took place. The totals for the merchandise selected will be added to the complete total for services and cash disbursements given to you before you were shown the merchandise.

Now is the time for you to change anything about the contract you do not like or are unable to understand. While making arrangements, you were considering each detail using the first criterion for getting what you want: "Is the funeral director acting in my best interest?" For example, did anything on that form present an inconvenience or a compromise you do not want to make? Is the total too high? The form found on pages 81–82 was prepared to indicate that you, as the consumer, were treated in accordance with the FTC rule currently in effect. (Possible changes may be required to comply with the revised rule.) It is also a legally binding note. Now ask yourself if the funeral director lived up to criterion number 2: "Am I comfortable with the alternatives I was offered?" Simply put, are you satisfied? And finally, criterion number 3: "What is my comfort level with the funeral director? Did he seem knowledgeable?"

Before signing the arrangement form, which has now become a contract, be sure you can afford it. A smart funeral director will assure himself that he will be paid. You should also expect him to ask you for payment of the "cash disbursements" prior to the interment.

A funeral is an event on a schedule. Once the funeral director has embalmed, he cannot unembalm. Once newspaper notices announcing the visiting hours and time of funeral service have been placed, people will schedule themselves to attend. Be sure the arrangements are what you want before you leave the funeral home.

As per the arrangements on the accompanying itemization #_____.

I/We who made the arrangements for the funeral do hereby attest to the following:

1. I/We were shown a General Price List, Casket Price List, and Outer Burial Container Price List effective this date prior to discussing the prices thereof.

2. I/We were not told that embalming is required by law and were told that the law does not require embalming except in certain special cases. If it was provided, it was done with our permission.

3. I/We were not told that any law requires embalming for direct cremations, immediate burial, a funeral using a sealed casket or if refrigeration is available and the funeral is without viewing or visitation and with a closed casket.

4. I/We were not told that any law requires a casket for direct cremation or that a casket other than an unfinished wood box is required for direct cremation or disposition.

5. I/We were told that state law does not require the purchase of an outer burial container or any of the funeral goods or services we select except as set forth on the statement of funeral goods and services I/we have selected.

6. No claims or warranties were made to me/us as to the merchandise or other offerings by this funeral home (embalming, casket, outer burial container), that embalming or the use of any merchandise available from this funeral home would delay the decomposition of the remains for the long term or an indefinite time, or would protect the body from gravesite substances. No representations or warranties were made to me/us about the protective features of caskets or outer containers other than those made by the manufacturers thereof. No other warranties were extended to me/us by the funeral home.

I/We hereby authorize the funeral home to provide the services arranged for, and represent that I am/we are the next of kin or am/are acting as duly authorized agent for the next of kin and hold the funeral home harmless from all consequences of my/our actions. I/We further authorize embalming, derma surgery, and/or pacemaker removal if deemed necessary by the funeral home.

I/We understand that this is an estimate not a bill, because there may be additional adjustments due to charges not specifically known to the Funeral Director at the time these arrangements are being authorized. They may include but are not limited to the following examples: adjustment of cash disbursements, overtime by suppliers, gratuities, flower delivery or disposal, additional service in obtaining the death certificate.

If this is a prearranged funeral, prices charged will be those in effect at time of need.

TERMS OF PAYMENT: The Funeral Supplier noted above holds the Estate of the Deceased and the undersigned jointly and severally responsible for full payment within 30 days. A deposit in the amount of $_____ is payable prior to burial or cremation. A discount in the amount of $_____ will be given for payment in full by _____ (date).

_____ L.S.   _____ address
_____ Funeral Director   _____ License #

PROMISSORY NOTE

For Value Received the undersigned promises to pay to the order of _____ the sum of _____ DOLLARS ($_____) on _____. The failure of the undersigned to make payment under the terms of this NOTE when due shall constitute default in the undersigned's obligation hereunder, and the holder hereof shall be entitled to collect against the undersigned in addition to the monies due hereunder all costs of collection including reasonable attorney's fees. In addition, in the event of such default, interest shall accrue on this NOTE at the rate of 1½% per month commencing on the first day following the due date hereof.

_____ L.S.   _____ address

9

Rip-Offs!

Several years ago in New Jersey there was a funeral director who found a unique way to rip people off. He billed people for a casket that was to be used to cremate their loved one, but when the body arrived at the crematory, it was in a cardboard box. The value of the casket purchased was $763, all pure profit for the funeral director. Prior to this, he had advertised for a funeral home that did not exist, thereby steering people to a facility he *did* have. This same individual tried to utilize another funeral director's funeral home knowing that he was out of town. When that failed, he called the wife of yet another funeral director and claimed he had permission to use that facility. He even had the family of the deceased go to that funeral home, without the owner's knowledge, and select a casket from his showroom!

Not yet finished, he managed to get convicted of failing to comply with the state rule of supplying each family with an itemization of what they had purchased, as well as misrepresenting the quality of the merchandise. Of course he also was convicted of practicing after he had lost his license.[1]

In California there was a funeral director whose escapades became the subject of a book.[2] To achieve such notoriety, it is claimed that he removed teeth containing dental gold, which he pawned, and internal organs, which he sold to an anatomical research bank, without the deceased family's knowledge. He also is alleged to have cremated many bodies at the same time while charging each consumer for an individual cremation, thus co-mingling the cremated remains for return to the families.

What both of these individuals have in common, aside from the obvious dishonesty, is that it was their fellow funeral directors who played a major role in bringing them to justice. I am convinced that funeral directors' business practices are the same as the business practices of people in any profession. There will always be bad apples, but what makes this type of activity so reprehensible in the funeral home profession is the vulnerability of the consumer who is using the services. Unfortunately, those bad apples are the ones responsible for creating legislation that burdens the ones who have done, and always will do, a creditable and ethical job of caring for people's needs.

Make no mistake about it, abuses do exist. But a consumer who is forewarned should not be overly concerned about using a funeral director's services. The purpose of this chapter is to give all consumers information that will cause bells to go off in the event of a potential abuse. The chapter is in two parts, the first being those abuses that are illegal or highly unethical. The second part presents the more insidious and subtle practices that have existed for a long time. They are not illegal, and many would argue that they are not unethical either. They are viewed by many as techniques that increase the amount of the sale. Ultimately they may turn the funeral experience into an even more unpleasant one than it already is. Remember that the purpose of the funeral is to have the disposition of the deceased accomplished in a way that has positive psychological results for the ones authorizing the services.

ILLEGAL OR HIGHLY UNETHICAL PRACTICES

Substitution of Merchandise

When you have selected the casket from among the many you are shown, you know the basic type, its color, and its price. When you arrive for viewing and see it again, how do you know it is the same casket?

Solution: The Federal Trade Commission requires a casket price list be in the consumer's presence when funeral arrangements are being made. But why not ask the funeral director when you have made the selection, for a copy of the descriptive invoice the casket is delivered with? Have him staple it to the completed copy of the arrangement contract. If you believe you have not been given what you selected, you now have the paperwork to check against the actual merchandise provided.

The same thing can be done with the burial vault. When you arrive at the grave site the vault is usually in the grave already. Sometimes the lid is displayed, sometimes it is not. Rarely is the casket placed in the vault above ground. As a funeral director, I always stayed to see the vault closed. I felt it was an act of kindness to have the family leave the grave before lowering the casket so that they would have a final remembrance of the casket and flowers.

Solution: Have a family representative stay also and have the funeral director point out to him the features of the vault.

Bait and Switch

This is easily done with floral pieces. The consumer is sold a specific arrangement for a set price. When it is displayed the flowers are of a less expensive variety or there are less of them, although the color and size of the container they are in is the same. Quite often this is the action of a florist rather than the funeral director. Most funeral directors could tell you which florists are habitual offenders. They can also tell you which florists tend to dump their older merchandise on the funeral purchaser. If you have one day of viewing and then the service, the flowers do not have to last long, do they?

Solution: When you order the flowers have the number and type of flowers specified on the order form. Order flowers in containers suitable to be taken home afterward. "Fireside baskets" and vases with dried arrangements fit that category.

Charging for Services Not Needed

Embalming is a prime example. According to the Federal Trade Commission, the consumer must authorize embalming prior to it taking place. If the deceased is to be viewed, embalming will most likely be required by the funeral director. In the case of a closed casket or an immediate cremation, embalming may not be necessary. There can be state rules governing the need to embalm. In New Jersey, for instance, burial, cremation, or embalming must take place with forty-eight hours after a deceased is removed from refrigeration.

Solution: Ask the funeral director why embalming is necessary.

The same thing can be done with the following items:

(a) The arrangement contract said "flower car" but you only had three floral pieces.

Solution: Cancel it. Remember, your arrangement contract states: "This is an estimate, not a bill." So as long as the service or merchandise was not provided, you cannot be billed for it.

(b) You were charged for a "holding room" because the services or visiting hours were not to take place until two days after the arrangements were made and the casketed deceased was kept there.

Solution: Whose delay was it? If Aunt Tilly was flying in for the services and you held things up, it is your burden; but if the funeral director could not have the room available, it is his. Don't pay.

(c) The funeral director says he needs pallbearers to carry the casket at the service and they cost $25 per person.

Solution: Ask if family or friends can carry it instead. In many cases these people would be honored to assist the family.

(d) You are being nickeled and dimed on prayer cards, thank you notes, register books, and clothing for the deceased.

Solution: Do you really need these items? Are they meaningful to you? In the case of clothing and thank you notes, you can probably get them yourself at a far more reasonable price.

(e) You are charged more for "cash disbursements" or money extended by the funeral director to third parties on the consumer's behalf than he actually paid out.

Solution: The Federal Trade Commission deals with this one also. The arrangement contract must contain a statement specifying that this is not the case. The funeral director must tell you if he has tacked on money for himself, or he is in violation.

The time to ask about these charges and alternatives is at the time the arrangement contract is being finalized. Sometimes just questioning the charge will get it taken off. If you are not sure of a charge, contact the place indicated as providing the service/merchandise and request a copy of the receipt.

SUBTLE PERSUASION

The second type of rip-off is much more subtle. It is not illegal, and, in fact, can stem from the funeral director's sincerity in believing in the services he provides. The majority can come from the funeral director's assumption that you need the recommendations he is making. *Make no mistake, funeral directors make their money by stressing the "traditional" funeral. They are not likely to offer you less expensive alternatives unless you ask for them.* And it's okay to ask for them. Remember, this is your purchase; your tastes and concerns (and the assumed wishes of the deceased), are what should determine your choices. Until the mid-1980s, consumers were likely to be given a "unit price" that took for granted that a traditional funeral with a service, limousine, and all the rest was wanted. The price would be given as a lump sum and the items it contained were listed but not itemized. When the individual states enacted regulations or the Federal Trade Commission promulgated its rule, "itemization" was in and "unit pricing" was out. Funeral directors quickly learned that they may have been giving away services under unit pricing. The need for itemization actually raised the price of the funeral for the smart funeral director, but it also gave the smart consumer the ability to reduce costs by reducing goods and services.

For a funeral director to keep the traditional funeral, and its price, he had to justify the cost. He did that by promoting the value of the traditional funeral. There is an entire language used that is more dignified than straightforward figures of speech.

I have already given the example in chapter 9 of funeral directors not using the word "embalm" when talking to a family who has just contacted them. The euphemism "prepare for viewing" sounds much more compassionate. We never talk about a dead body, but we do discuss the "deceased." Where is the line crossed between kindness and respect on the one hand and creating an atmosphere of deception on the other? When a funeral director makes not so subtle statements about the need to honor the deceased by doing things in the memory of your loved one, the line has definitely been crossed.

Funerals are for the living, and the funeral director earns his fees by selling goods and services appropriate to the needs of the survivors. The consumer cannot expect the funeral home business person to urge the purchase of less expensive services and merchandise if the consumer has expressly asked for the more expensive services and merchandise. At the same time, the funeral director has no right to make the family feel guilty for trying to be practical, thereby nudging them toward a higher-priced funeral. There are occasions when a funeral director may actually try to talk a family out of certain purchases. As I had repeat funerals within the same families, I began to know the people well. I knew the ones who could not afford to spend the money, and I usually found a way to accommodate them. I also wanted assurances that the bill would be paid. When I retired I had a drawer full of unpaid bills from the days when my grandfather, my mother, and I were not so consumer oriented. *Consumerism is a two-way street.*

Here are some common ways the funeral director can increase your desire to spend more:

1. If the funeral director uses phrases like, "This is the final tribute you can give to your father," or "You only have one chance to do this right for Mom," bells and whistles should go off in your head. You are being told that you should think nothing of spending more money. You are being encouraged to consider merchandise and services you would not have thought about before you were in the funeral director's presence.

   Solution: Keep in mind that the funeral service is for the living. Use the trend toward itemization of the services and thoughtful consumerism to create a service that is particularly meaningful. Your young child won't care what you paid for her grandpa's casket, but she may have a lasting impression from having been allowed to read a poem about what Grandpa meant to her. A good rule of thumb is that personal touches have meaning to the living. Placing favorite pictures in the casket can be far more poignant and lasting than buying a $200 casket floral piece.

2. The consumer is not shown an inexpensive casket. The funeral director is not under obligation to offer the minimum casket available. I know of casket display rooms where the minimum available costs more than three times the minimum I had on display. There are available caskets with interiors suitable for viewing for well under $200 (wholesale). The funeral director will sell one to you for between $400 and $600 on a normal markup. But if you don't know he has it, you can't purchase it. If he wants to keep you in a traditional funeral where he can make money on other charges, he will probably sell you that minimum casket at close to cost if asked.

Solution: The Federal Trade Commission requires that the caskets offered for sale be prominently displayed on a list when you are making arrangements. If you see no casket suitable for viewing for under $400, find out why.

3. You start hearing claims like this: a particular burial vault is "waterproof" or provides more protection than another model, or "this casket will last longer."

Solution: It is against FTC regulations for the funeral director to make warranties without written proof. Ask to see the relevant warranties for caskets and/or vaults to determine their truth.

4. The funeral director prolongs the process. Yes, in the old days it was not unusual to have several days of viewing and then a service. But do you really need it? When the funeral director's preparation has been done and the casketed body is ready for viewing, additional facility charges are just extra income.

Solution: You pay for what you use. Only the consumer should decide how much time is needed at the funeral facility. It is better to leave a day in between the day you make the arrangements and the service or viewing, than to have two days at the funeral home with no one there the first day because no one knew about the death.

This chapter has touched on the rip-offs. Remember that you can avoid almost all of them by having a solid knowledge of the material in chapter 8. There, each item on the arrangement contract is broken down with options and cost markups. *Above all,* funeral directors are required by the Federal Trade Commission to give their prices over the phone or supply a written list of charges and available merchandise upon request. You can price shop. If you do that, your chances of being taken advantage of are slim.

NOTES

1. Department of Law and Public Safety, State of New Jersey, Division of Consumer Affairs, Board of Mortuary Science (March 26, 1981).
2. Ken Englade, *A Family Business* (New York: St. Martin's, 1992).

10

The Prearranged Funeral

Prearranged funerals, those arranged prior to the time of need, can provide tremendous advantages to consumers and funeral directors alike. Remember that I highly recommended taking along a person emotionally removed from the death, someone able to think critically, when making funeral arrangements. An unemotional thinker is protection not only from spending too much money, but also from making decisions that can affect how satisfying the funeral is for those who grieve. The observer may think of additional details that need to be attended to or alternatives that a grieving person might find comforting. Prearrangements, particularly for one's own funeral, allow for that logical, less emotional thought. They are particularly beneficial to peace of mind. The disposition of the remains and the nature of the funeral are controlled by the person whose memory will be recalled by those attending and so the funeral is literally "the way he or she would have wanted it." The arrangements allow for the planning of all the concerns one has about how his or her death will be handled. Any questions, alternative ideas, or loose ends can be cleared up comfortably without rushing into anything.

It was not unusual for me to see several families a week who wanted to make prearrangements. One of my funeral homes was in a retirement area. There were files full of these prearranged funerals, and some literally sat on file for twenty years. If your funeral home of preference is sold, there is usually no need to worry. If the funerals are prepaid, then, much like a lease arrangement, if the funeral home is sold, the prearranged funerals are sold with it. Many of these retirees knew us well from our other funeral homes. It was a standing joke with them that the first week they were in their retirement home, they transferred their assets to the new area, bought a cemetery plot, prearranged their funeral, and then spent the next couple of decades having a great time.

It also makes sense to prearrange the funeral of a person you are responsible for who may be terminally ill. Finding vital information when death occurs suddenly can be a frustrating experience. Ask yourself: what are Mom's and Dad's Social Security numbers and their dates of birth? In what cemetery will your parents be buried? I heard many people breathe a huge sigh of relief when, after being left in charge of the affairs of a person who had just died, they called the funeral home as instructed and were told that complete preplanned arrangements had been signed by the deceased.

Prearranging a funeral can be taken to any stage of completion desired. But funeral wishes do no good if they are not readily available when needed. A person's "will" is not the place to outline funeral wishes. Usually wills are found and read several days after the interment, at which time the deceased's burial wishes are irrelevant. Preplanning takes three forms: the simplest is just jotting down some basic wishes to be followed when death occurs. On a slightly more sophisticated level, these wishes can then be filed with a funeral director, lawyer, or someone who will be in charge of the funeral. Lastly, the funeral can be prepaid. We will consider the pros and cons of these three alternatives.

WRITE DOWN YOUR WISHES

This is an excellent idea for the reasons stated in the first paragraph of this chapter. Knowing what you want done with your remains and how you would like the funeral conducted makes things so much easier for those left behind. In addition, it is very healthy to think about that death occurring. Without delving into psychology too deeply, thoughts about your own death and the ability to consider those thoughts indicate an acceptance, which can make it easier. Of course, dwelling on death can be morbid, but it was my experience when making prearrangements with people that it was not a morbid experience for them. As described above, it was a relief. This is the least complex of our three scenarios.

FILE PREARRANGEMENTS WITH A
FUNERAL DIRECTOR OR LAWYER

I once knew a woman who lived all alone and who kept the funeral arrangements she had made with me hanging in a picture frame in her bedroom. Her thinking was that if she died at home, whoever found her would be bound to see the arrangements and call the funeral home! She was a great person with a terrific sense of humor, but even as comfortable with death as I am, I am not sure that I would want my funeral arrangements hanging over my bed!

Placing your funeral wishes in your "will" does little good. They need to be where they can be readily found at the time of need. For most folks, leaving their vital information and funeral requests on file with the funeral director of choice probably makes more sense. If you have taken the time and effort to write them out, why not have the additional peace of mind that selecting the funeral home would provide? You do not incur any obligation to the funeral home by leaving your records there and you could be saving your relatives, or whoever is handling your estate, a lot of aggravation. The alternative is to leave the plans with a lawyer, your designated executor (executrix), or the person you want in charge and let him or her choose the funeral home.

PREPAYING A PREARRANGED FUNERAL

Of the three alternatives, prepaying requires the most discussion because it can present the most problems for the consumer. While prearrangements reduce the confusion for relatives who may not have been certain what the deceased wanted, and make it easier for the funeral director to do his job, by now we should realize that funerals are big business. As pointed out in chapter 1, there is a company trading on the New York Stock Exchange that owns nothing but funeral homes, related florists, and cemeteries.[1] Just as a hint of how popular prepaid prearrangements are, in 1981 the New Jersey State Funeral Directors Association reached an agreement with a bank to set up a Prepaid Trust Fund. By 1992 it was up to $59 million in assets.[2] This is only one of the vehicles through which prepayment can be made, and it is only for the State of New Jersey.

An excellent way for the funeral director to tap into the potential market is to promote "prearrangements." With the New Jersey Trust Fund, the individual funeral directors set up the arrangements at their specific homes, and the trust holds the money. The contract form goes with the payment to the trust, but the amount put in can be any amount (over $500) that the consumer chooses. The person who prepays can move the arrangements to any funeral home at any time without transferring the money. At the time of need, the money is automatically drawn by the funeral home. This can be a major advantage since estates take time to settle and funds can be tied up. The funds may be withdrawn at any time, along with the interest that has accrued, by the party who arranged the funeral. Because these prepayments are with a bank, they are insured by the federal government, and they earn a comparatively high interest because they are pooled funds. A prepaid arrangement of this type is about the best vehicle if the consumer is looking for safety, a good rate of return on the investment, and convenience. Unfortunately, regulations regarding prepaid trusts vary from state to state. In discussing the matter with the National Funeral Directors Association (NFDA), Milwaukee, Wisconsin, they pointed out that at one time they administered a program for prepayment, but now they leave it to the individual states because of the separate state regulations. The NFDA can advise consumers regarding the appropriate state office or agency to call to ascertain a specific state's regulations.

There can be one enormous advantage to prepaying funeral funds into an *irrevocable trust*. I would not ordinarily recommend not being able to retrieve your money if the need arises, but under Social Security Medicaid regulations, a consumer may set aside funeral/burial expenses and not include them in their declared assets, provided the funds can not be used for any other purpose. That way the funds for funeral/burial expenses are available when other resources have been exhausted (due to nursing home stays, protracted hospital stays, or prolonged illness) and do not affect a person's Medicaid status.* These Medicaid regulations recently changed. Check the current regulations at the time you are considering this option.

An alternative to the prepaying of funeral expenses is maintaining an individual bank account. These can be made payable to a specific funeral director, in which case they solve the problem of having funds immediately available at the time of service, but are not as likely to pay a high rate of interest. The consumer is also at the mercy of the funeral home that set it up and the bank chosen. *Be certain the account is set up "in trust" for your funeral expenses. That way the funeral home can not draw on the funds unless proof of death is supplied to the bank.* As this volume goes to press, the new Federal Trade Commission Rule has yet to be published. When it is made public I think it is likely that the rule will not permit prepaid funds to be in the name of the funeral director (see the Appendix).

---

*Medicaid status is based on one's income and assets. Those with assets above a particular minimum are not eligible for Medicaid.

Another alternative is "life insurance." When life insurance first was devised it was called "death insurance." In a burst of marketing genius, the insurance industry thought "life insurance" sounded better. Check with insurance salespeople for the types available. Some may pay higher dividends than a trust account. However, some are not insured. If the company goes under, what happens to your money? These same companies can issue annuities that serve the same basic function: they provide an annual payment to the beneficiary.

When you are thinking of prepaying, consider where the "sell" is coming from. Funeral directors are paid a commission if they enroll you in an insurance plan just as any insurance salesperson would be. It is the case in New Jersey that the funeral directors association receives an "administration fee" as a percentage of the pre-need funds they collect.

If you prepay, be careful! Ask yourself these questions:

1. Who holds the funds and are they insured?

2. Can I change the plans, the designated funeral home, and the amount of money in the account whenever I want?

3. Am I protected from those who could abuse the funds while on deposit or in escrow?

Be suspicious of prepaid funeral arrangements that guarantee services and specific merchandise at today's prices, regardless of how far in the future death occurs. Read the fine print. For instance, what if a particular casket is no longer available at the time of need? What if you move?

Pre-need planning can serve important personal requirements, but only if tailored to meet specific needs.

NOTES

1. Service Corporation International (See footnote 2, chapter 1).
2. New Jersey State Funeral Directors Association.

11

The Funeral Arrangement Checklist Applicable to Your Own Funeral or When Arranging Someone Else's

PRE-NEED

1. Determine what your needs are by deciding on what basic type of service you want. Discuss the potential service with the people closest to you. Do these needs include:

   A. the traditional funeral as prescribed by the funeral rites of the applicable religion;

   B. a variation of the above to more closely suit personal needs;

   C. burial or cremation;

   D. the location where disposition will take place?

2. Shop for a funeral director by using the cost of the goods and services as a criterion for selection, or stay with a familiar funeral director and seek the best deal you can.

3. Write down your wishes and be as specific as possible about actual goods and services, including price ranges.

   A. Give those wishes to someone who will make the arrangements at the time of need (your next of kin, the executor [executrix] of your estate, etc.).

   B. If you choose, leave a signed copy of the arrangements with the funeral director who is likely to handle the services.

C. In some circumstances, you may wish to prepay for the prearrangements.

D. At the very least, prepare a list of vital information about yourself or the person for whom you are making the arrangements.

E. Have a person designated who knows he or she is in charge of the funeral.

AT THE TIME OF NEED: NOW THERE IS A TIME SCHEDULE

1. When the hospital, nursing home, doctor, police, or medical authority notifies the next of kin or the person in charge of funeral arrangements that a death has occurred, the party notified is usually urged to contact a funeral director. Either call a funeral home you know and seek the best financial deal possible, or price shop by phone to find a funeral home you are comfortable with. You'll probably remember local funeral homes that saw to the needs of friends, workmates, or other family members. If none come to mind, then contact a friend or two for possible referrals. Don't forget, there's always the yellow pages.

A. If the funeral is an immediate cremation or burial with no attendant services, the overriding factor is cost.

B. If there are services, combine the "comfort factor" of the funeral director you may select with price considerations.

2. Authorize the funeral director to remove the deceased and bring the body to the funeral home.

A. If there will be visiting and calling hours to view the body, authorize embalming.

B. If there will *not be* viewing, make it clear that you do not want embalming.

3. Go to the funeral home at the time you mutually agreed to meet with the funeral director.

A. Have your specific wishes for the funeral firmly in mind.

B. Bring the vital information on the deceased, including any cemetery deeds or authorizations.

    C. Bring the newspaper information, particularly relatives' names and addresses, written down.

    D. Bring the clothing that will be worn; in the case of a woman who has died, provide her own makeup. If a wig or toupee was worn by the deceased, bring that as well.

    E. Bring someone who is relatively unemotional about the death unless you are sure you can make business decisions on your own.

4. Having made the funeral arrangements, call those who should know about the death.

5. Attend to any funeral details the funeral director is not handling for you (for example, personal cars, a gathering after the funeral, etc.).

6. Tie up any loose business ends such as procuring the will, locating life insurance policies, and the like. You will probably be limited in your access to the deceased's financial affairs until the estate has been legally probated (unless you are the executor [executrix]). In some cases, this process can be done prior to the funeral services if you wish, but many people prefer to have the funeral over first. If you are emotionally close to the deceased, use the funeral for its designated purpose, mourning. Then, after the final disposition, take care of business.

7. If no executor (executrix) was established, or if the deceased died without making a will (dying intestate), then you may wish to seek help in settling the estate of the person who has died. A lawyer is the most obvious source, or call the surrogate's court to determine how to handle the estate.

8. If you were emotionally attached to the person who died, monitor how the loss is affecting you. If you need help, contact an organization specific to your needs. For example, if you lost a child, seek out that group of parents who has suffered a loss that is similar to yours. Often, shared experiences help a great deal. If that is not enough, seek out friends or clergy you are close to or, if need be, professional counselors or therapists who are qualified to deal with your problem.

12

Frequently Asked Questions

1. What benefits are available to help pay for the funeral?

Much less outside help is now available then was the case just a few years ago. But as of this writing the following applies:

Veterans Administration: No cash benefit is paid unless the deceased was on disability. Burial is allowed in some designated national cemeteries with grave space provided for veterans with other than a dishonorable discharge. Arlington National Cemetery is only available to active military, retired military, purple heart and silver star recipients and others who have been decorated. A grave marker is available for veterans not buried in private cemeteries.

Social Security: A minimum benefit of $255 is available for spouses living with the deceased or the dependent child of the deceased.

SSI/Medicaid: No burial funds are provided. By setting up an irrevocable prepaid funeral trust, assets can be set aside for the funeral which do not affect the person's Medicaid status.

Check these agencies at the time of need.

2. What happens to the embalming waste?

It is estimated that a human body with a weight of 100 pounds will generate 7.43 pounds of flushed fluids during an embalming. A 200-pound body will generate 10.2 pounds of fluids. Depending on local and state regulations, the fluids from the body are generally allowed to run down the drain. There are guidelines for treating infectious waste which call for mixing it with formaldehyde solutions prior to this method of disposal. A tightening of federal and local laws is limiting the ability of funeral directors to continue using this method. In many places this can not be done where a septic system is in use. There is at least one community that specifically targeted funeral homes and precluded them from discharge into the municipal sewer system. If a holding tank is used, it must be pumped out by a medical waste hauler.

Solid waste in the form of sheets, gauze, and "sharps" (i.e., needles generated by healthcare providers prior to the death) often end up in the hands of the funeral directors. Stringent laws now call for logs to be kept of embalmings, and the disposal of this medical waste by licensed medical waste haulers. Funeral directors must be constantly concerned with the hazards of exposure to infectious disease and the demands of medical waste requirements, all of which can drive up the cost to the consumer. The Occupational Safety and Health Administration's specific safety requirements for the workplace and other federal regulations, including the Americans with Disabilities Act, which apply to most funeral home facilities, have driven up the costs of the facilities tremendously.

3. It seems like I never see any cars around some funeral homes. How many funerals do most funeral homes handle?

The nation's average for number of services handled by each funeral home is 158 per year. Of course some handle more, some less, and the number can vary tremendously depending on whether the funeral home is rural, suburban, or city. Bear in mind that if a funeral home has a traditional funeral in progress with visiting and a funeral service outside the funeral home, people will be there generally in the afternoon and evening, and briefly in the morning.

4. I went to a Catholic funeral the other day and could not believe that they actually had a cremation after the mass. How long has this been going on?

The trend in funerals is toward a service that truly serves the economic and spiritual needs of the survivors. In reality, that is what the funeral experience should be about. Traditional religious rites are being relaxed to some extent with all the major religions. The religious requirements may vary not only from religion to religion, but also from church to church, temple to temple, and clergy to clergy. For some survivors, these religious requirements are very important; for others they are not. The consumer should check with the religious authority that applies to his or her particular case. In this instance, cremation is allowed for a Catholic under some circumstances and can hold down the cost of the interment considerably while satisfying the requirements of the church.

5. Why did I pay a separate fee for the "preparation room" and then another fee for "use of a chapel" and yet another charge for a "room for visitation"?

By fully itemizing the use, or nonuse, of each available item on the arrangement contract form, the consumer has the advantage of being able to hold down costs. If there was no visiting, there would have been no charge for a "room for visitation." Visitation that is one day in length should not cost as much as visitation that is two days. Selecting less service or merchandise results in lower cost. This is known as "itemization." It replaces "unit pricing" (the whole funeral as a package or unit) which lumps charges together and does not allow for as much flexibility in holding down costs.

6. Why does a funeral cost so much money?

A funeral does not have to cost much money. Of course some funeral wishes *do* cost a lot of money. To hold down the cost, first consider what is really needed and try to stay away from the "traditional" American funeral with lengthy visiting in the funeral home. Immediate burial or cremation is the least expensive, but will it meet the consumer's needs? The answer probably lies somewhere between the full-service traditional funeral and immediate burial or cremation. Consider a type of funeral that is personally satisfying to psychological and financial needs. The funeral director has the tools to give you options. That is a funeral director's true value to the consumer. It has been my goal in this book to help the consumer ask the right questions of the funeral director.

The second part of the answer lies with funeral director's costs of operation. How palatial is the funeral home? You are helping to pay for it and the overhead it generates when you utilize the funeral director's services. The funeral director has escalating costs due to increased government regulation of the facilities that must be made available, disposal of medical waste, and professional requirements. Better service can not be provided without additional costs of operation, and the funeral director is being mandated to provide more options to the consumer.

7. I see all types of grave markers. What do they cost?

There are two types of grave markers: ones that lie flat on the ground and those that are upright. "Memorial Parks" have the flat on-the-ground type of markers. This allows for easier maintenance of the cemetery; the grass can be cut by running over the top. Upright markers are more traditional, however. Whereas the flat markers can be bronze or stone, most upright markers are granite or marble. The flat markers are much less expensive, usually a standard size, and set into a concrete base. The cost can be as little as several hundred dollars. Upright markers can be very fancy in design and quite costly. They will start in price higher than the flat markers and their upper range is limited only by the consumer's desires.

8. Why have an open casket? I think it's barbaric.

There are sound psychological reasons for an open casket in some circumstances. Refer to Elisabeth Kubler-Ross and her breakthrough studies on death and dying (see the resource bibliography). Essentially, the grieving process can not begin until there is an acceptance that death has occurred. Confronting the death in the form of an open casket helps to bring about that acceptance. In cases of sudden death where the friends and relatives were not present, an open casket may be very beneficial. The same is true for accident victims. When someone who has played a significant part in our lives simply disappears from our existence, the healing process can take longer to begin, if it begins at all. Viewing the body can help that emotional healing to start.

9. I don't believe in funerals. Why have anything?

First and foremost, a funeral recognizes that there has been a life. It is as important to the lives of others as a wedding or an anniversary. As I said earlier, funerals are not for the dead, but for the living. A funeral need not be complicated or expensive and should be tailored to the specific consumer's needs. Feeling as you do, you would probably opt for a very simple funeral if someone close to you dies. Perhaps nothing more than an appropriate burial or cremation with a short prayer (if you are at all religious) is in order.

Above: In the nineteenth century (1853), caskets were often obtained from local furniture makers, some of whom began to "undertake" the responsibility of conducting the funerals.

Below: Later (1914), as funeral arranging became more of a profession, the funeral director emerged, along with a free-standing facility to prepare the deceased, hold visiting hours, and conduct the funeral service.

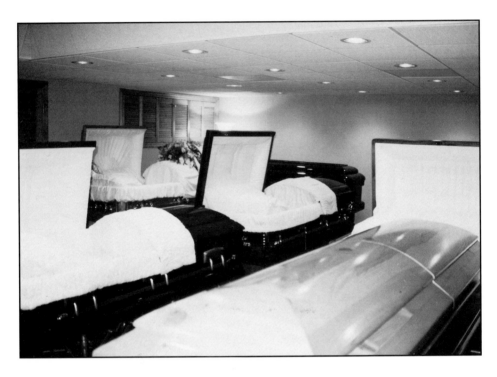

After the funeral arrangement conference, the funeral director should conduct the consumer into the casket display room to choose the casket most appropriate for the survivors' needs.

The choice—of model (i.e., sealed, unsealed, full-open, partially open, with or without rails or handles, etc.); materials (wood, metal, or fiber glass); and interior (i.e., fabric, cushioning, spring mattress, etc.)—is a very personal one that only the consumer can and should make once all information about the materials and pricing have been provided.

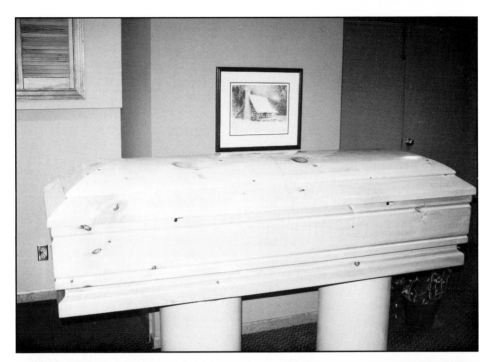

Above: A basic wooden casket: a simple, plain pine construction with no hardware (rails or handles) and no ornate decorations.

Below: A good-quality oak casket with wooden handlerails, decorative woodwork, and attractive lining. These represent a sampling of the range of available caskets.

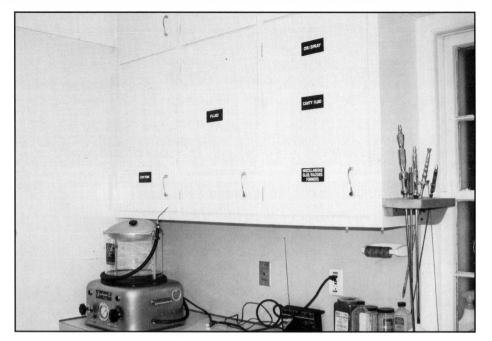

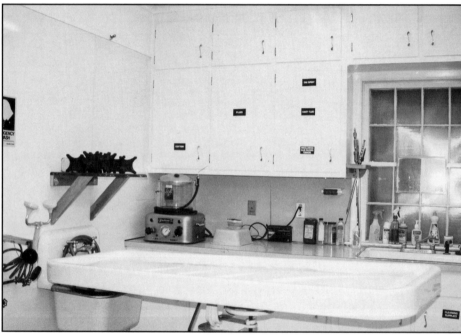

Above: A close-up of a contemporary funeral director's embalming machine, with trocars hanging in a nearby rack. This area also houses all needed surgical instruments, many of which resemble those of physicians.

Below: A contemporary embalming room containing the embalming table, the embalming machine, and related supplies. These facilities are inspected by appropriate state licensing agencies and the federal OSHA regulators. Concern for chemical exposure and waste disposal, along with control of infectious diseases, has forced the upgrading of the preparation room.

10. I sometimes see young children at funerals. They are usually running around. Why would anyone take young children to a funeral in the first place?

It is my experience that adults who were exposed to funerals when they were children tend to accept death and dying as a part of life more easily than those who did not have that experience. But children must be exposed to it properly. Realize that if the whole family is going to visiting hours or to a funeral, children old enough to understand where the adults are going will feel left out and excluded. If the children do not know the deceased, then some explanation will need to be given. If, however, the children know the person who has died, then they, too, have the need to experience the parting. The reason children are usually running around at a funeral home is that they are kids and they are resilient. Once they feel comfortable with the situation, they revert to the normal behavior of children. I always advised people bringing children to a funeral to do the following:

1. Unless the children are able to ask questions and understand explanations, do not expose youngsters to a body in a casket. The very young can still be a part of the process by being with relatives and friends, but not in direct contact with the deceased.

2. When children are old enough to miss the loss of a person they knew, they should have a chance to accept the death. Tell them exactly what they are going to see. For instance: "There is a large room and when we walk in you will see rows of chairs and people, some of whom you know. At the front will be a lot of flowers around a casket. Do you know what a casket is? Grandma is lying down inside the casket. The people are there because she has died and they loved her and want to have a chance to remember her. What you see is the "shell" that the Grandma you knew lived in. The part of Grandma that talked to you and had fun tickling you has gone to be with God (or is now a very special part of all of us who knew her). Grandma isn't in that body anymore. So the people who loved her, like you do, are here to say goodbye, and we wanted you to be a part of that."

3. Don't ever say: "Grandma is just sleeping." To children, that can be a devastating thought. Some will think, "Am I going to go to sleep and never wake up?"

"We are going to bury Grandma's body in the ground." Once the children know the only part of Grandma that remains is the body, which has separated from the soul (or essence) that lives on, then they can accept the "shell" being buried. But, I would not try to take a young child to the cemetery or to the crematorium.

4. Do not surprise a child with a body in a casket. Do not make the child go near the casket if he or she does not want to do so. Do not make a child touch the body, and do not force the child go to the funeral if he or she does not want to. Certainly do not leave the child with someone at the funeral who does not know how you have handled the situation.

11. I joined a memorial society when I was living out West. How much less expensive is the funeral?

Be careful about joining associations that claim to reduce the cost of funerals. Do they provide the funeral service and therefore directly control the costs? If they have arrangements with funeral homes, what happens if you are not in an area where those funeral homes are located? If you desire to purchase the least expensive method of disposition available, can you get it more reasonably by looking in the yellow pages and making a few phone calls at the time the death occurs? It is my personal feeling that memorial societies served a purpose before funerals became more consumer oriented. Now, pricing and information is directly available from the funeral directors themselves.

Resource Bibliography

For those seeking more information on specific subjects related to funerals and their cost, I have provided some useful sources. Books or other materials focusing, in whole or in part, on the cost of a funeral or on legal requirements should have a publication date of 1984 or later. Books written prior to 1984 are not recommended since it was in that year that the Federal Trade Commission's rule was adopted, which had a major impact on the industry. Please note: this caution does not apply to books or publications on the subject of funeral rites or customs and related matters (i.e., grieving, widowhood, etc.).

FUNERAL RITES

Bernardin, Joseph B. *Burial Services.* Harrisburg, Penn.: Morehouse Publishing, 1980.

Brendann, Effie. *Death Customs: An Analytical Study of Burial Rites.* Detroit, Mich.: Omnigraphics, Inc., 1972.

Cadenhead, Al, Jr. *The Ministers Manual for Funerals.* Nashville, Tenn.: Broadman. 1988.

Carlson, Lisa. *Caring for Your Own Dead.* Hinebgurg, Vt.: Upper Access Publishers, 1987.

Ford, Josephine M. *The Silver Lining: Personalized Scriptural Wake Services.* Mystic, Conn.: Twenty Third Publications, 1987.

Lamont, Corliss. *The Humanist Funeral Service.* Buffalo, N.Y.: Prometheus Books, 1977.

Marchal, Michael. *Parish Funerals: A Guide to the Order of Christian Funerals.* Chicago, Ill.: Liturgy Training Publications, 1987.

Martin, Edward A. *A Psychology of Funeral Service*. Arlington, Va.: E. A. Martin Publishing, 1987.

Morgan, Ernest. *Dealing Creatively with Death: A Manual of Death Education and Simple Burial*. Burnsville, N.C.: Celo Press, 1990.

Rabinowitz, Tzui. *A Guide to Life: Jewish Laws and Customs of Mourning*. Dunsmores, Penn.: Aronson, 1989.

Rutherford, Richard. *Death of a Christian: Rite of Funerals*. New York: Pueblo Pub. Co., 1990. (Studies in the reformed rites of the Catholic Church.)

Wynne Willson, Jane. *Funerals without God: A Practical Guide to Non-Religious Funerals*. Buffalo, N.Y.: Prometheus Books, 1990.

GRIEVING

Grollman, Earl A. *Living When a Loved One Had Died*. Boston, Mass.: Beacon Press, 1987.

James, John W., and Frank Cherry. *The Grief Recovery Handbook: A Step-By-Step Program for Moving Beyond Loss*. New York: Harper Row, 1989.

Kubler-Ross, Elisabeth. *On Death and Dying*. New York: Macmillan Publishing Company, 1982.

Lightner, Candy, and Nancy Hathaway. *Giving Sorrow Words: How to Cope with Grief and Get on with Your Life*. New York: Warner Books, 1990.

Marshall, George N. *Facing Death and Grief: A Sensible Perspective for the Modern Person*. Buffalo, N.Y.: Prometheus Books, 1981.

Rando, Theresa. *Grieving: How to Go on Living When Someone You Love Dies*. Champaign, Ill.: Res Press, 1988. (Also discusses funeral ritual ideas for personalization of the process. The author has several other titles dealing with specific areas of grief.)

Tatlebaum, Judy. *Courage to Grieve*. New York: Harper Row, 1990.

ORGANIZATIONS FOR FUNERAL INFORMATION

A word of caution: The organizations representing specific groups are likely to have a definite point of view. Their information can be extremely helpful, but should be read with a critical eye.

American Association of Retired Persons, 1909 K Street N.W., Washington, D.C. 20049

American Cemetery Association, 3 Skyline Place, Suite 1111, 5201 Leesburg Pike, Falls Church, VA 22041

The American Humanist Association, 7 Harwood Drive, Amherst, NY 14226

Committee for Democratic and Secular Humanism, 3965 Rensch Road, Amherst, NY 14226

Continental Association of Funeral and Memorial Societies, 7910 Woodmont Avenue, Suite 1208, Bethesda, MD 20814

Cremation Association of North America, 111 East Wacker Drive, Chicago, IL 60601

National Funeral Directors Association, 11121 West Oklahoma Avenue, Milwaukee, WI 53227

ANATOMICAL GIFTS

Medic Alert Foundation, P.O. Box 1009, Turlock, CA 95381-1009

United Network of Organ Sharing, 1100 Boulders Parkway, Suite 500, Richmond, VA 23225-8770

ORGANIZATIONS FOR POST-FUNERAL HELP

American Association of Retired Persons, 1909 K Street, N.W., Washington, D.C. 20049 (Direct your inquiry to the Widowed Persons Service; literature available.)

Committee for Democratic and Secular Humanism, 3965 Rensch Road, Amherst, NY 14226

The Compassionate Friends, 900 Jorie Boulevard, Oak Brook, IL 60521 (Self-help group for parents who must come to terms with the death of a child. Local chapters: I highly recommend them from my experience as a funeral director.)

Elisabeth Kubler-Ross Center, South Route 616, Head Waters, VA 24442

National Hospice Organization, 1901 North Moore Street, Suite 901, Arlington, VA 22209 (Provides information on support groups and local hospice care for the terminally ill.)

National Sudden Infant Death Syndrome Foundation, 10500 Little Patuxent Parkway, Suite 420, Columbia, MD 21044

THEOS Foundation, 717 Liberty Avenue, Pittsburgh, PA 15301 (Mutual support for widowed persons; maintains local chapters.)

FUNERAL SERVICE COMPLAINTS

Funeral Service Consumer Assistance Program, National Research and Information Center, 1614 Central Street, Evanston, IL 60201 (Originally set up under a different name by the National Funeral Directors Association to hear complaints, it was spun off as an independent agency because the funeral directors wanted it to be neutral in the complaint process.)

Cemetery Consumer Service Council, P.O. Box 3574, Washington, D.C. 20007 (Sponsored by five trade groups within the cemetery industry, it maintains representatives in each state who will mediate for the consumer and cemetery to seek solutions.)

U.S. Federal Trade Commission, 6th and Pennsylvania N.W., Washington, D.C. 20580 (Hears complaints on violations of the rule relating to funeral homes. Refers others to FSCAP [above].)

If these organizations can not rectify a particular situation, recourse can be found through the appropriate state agency. Legal redress can be sought through the attorney general's Consumer Affairs Division or the funeral directors' professional licensing board.

COMPREHENSIVE OVERVIEW OF DEATH AND DYING

Anderson, Patricia. *Affairs in Order: A Complete Resource Guide to Death and Dying.* New York: Macmillan Publishing Company, 1991. (An excellent book for an overview of many issues surrounding preparation for death.)

Federal Trade Commission (FTC)
Trade Regulation Rule,* 1984
Part 453: Funeral Industry Practices

SECTION 453.1 DEFINITIONS

(a) *Accounting year.* "Accounting year" refers to the particular calendar year or other one year period used by a funeral provider in keeping financial records for tax or accounting purposes.

(b) *Alternative container.* An "alternative container" is a nonmetal receptacle or enclosure, without ornamentation or a fixed interior lining, which is designed for the encasement of human remains and which is made of cardboard, pressed-wood, composition materials (with or without an outside covering) or pouches of canvas or other materials.

(c) *Cash advance item.* A "cash advance item" is any item of service or merchandise described to a purchaser as a "cash advance," "accommodation," "cash disbursement," or similar term. A cash advance item is also any item obtained from a third party and paid for by the funeral provider on the purchaser's behalf. Cash advance items may include, but are not limited to, the following items: cemetery or crematory services; pallbearers; public transportation; clergy honoraria; flowers; musicians or singers; nurses; obituary notices; gratuities; and death certificates.

---

*At the time this book went to press, the "rule" had just been revised by the FTC. The 1984 rule remains in effect until July 19, 1994, at which time the provisions of the new rule will apply.

(d) *Casket.* A "casket" is a rigid container which is designed for the encasement of human remains and which is usually constructed of wood, metal, or like material, and ornamented and lined with fabric.

(e) *Commission.* "Commission" refers to the Federal Trade Commission.

(f) *Cremation.* "Cremation" is a heating process which incinerates human remains.

(g) *Crematory.* A "crematory" is any person, partnership, or corporation that performs cremation and sells funeral goods.

(h) *Direct cremation.* A "direct cremation" is a disposition of human remains by cremation, without formal viewing, visitation, or ceremony with the body present.

(i) *Funeral goods.* "Funeral goods" are the goods which are sold or offered for sale directly to the public for use in connection with funeral services.

(j) *Funeral provider.* A "funeral provider" is any person, partnership, or corporation that sells or offers to sell funeral goods and funeral services to the public.

(k) *Funeral services.* "Funeral services" are any services which may be used to care for and prepare deceased human bodies for burial, cremation, or other final disposition; and arrange, supervise, or conduct the funeral ceremony or the final disposition of deceased human bodies.

(l) *Immediate burial.* An "immediate burial" is a disposition of human remains by burial, without formal viewing, visitation, or ceremony with the body present, except for a graveside service.

(m) *Outer burial container.* An "outer burial container" is any container which is designed for placement in the grave around the casket including, but not limited to, containers commonly known as burial vaults, grave boxes, and grave liners.

(n) *Person.* A "person" is any individual, partnership, corporation, association, government or governmental subdivision or agency, or other entity.

(o) *Services of funeral director and staff.* The "services of funeral director and staff" are the services, not included in prices of other categories in Section 453.2(b)(4) [below] which may be furnished by a funeral provider in arranging and supervising a funeral, such as conducting the arrangements conference, planning the funeral, obtaining necessary permits, and placing obituary notices.

(p) *Unfinished wood box.* An "unfinished wood box" is an unornamented casket made of wood which does not have a fixed interior lining.

SECTION 453.2 PRICE DISCLOSURES

(a) Unfair or deceptive acts or practices. In selling or offering to sell funeral goods or funeral services to the public, it is an unfair or deceptive act or practice for a funeral provider to fail to furnish price information disclosing the cost to the purchaser for each of the specific funeral goods and funeral services used in connection with the disposition of deceased human bodies, including at least the price of embalming, transportation of remains, use of facilities, caskets, outer burial containers, immediate burials, or direct cremations, to persons inquiring about the purchase of funerals. Any funeral provider who complies with the preventative requirements in paragraph (b) of this section is not engaged in the unfair or deceptive acts or practices defined here.

(b) Preventative requirements. To prevent these unfair or deceptive acts or practices, as well as the unfair or deceptive acts or practices defined in Section 453.4(b)(1) [below], funeral providers must:

1. Telephone Price Disclosures.

    (i) Tell persons who call the funeral provider's place of business and ask about the terms, conditions, or prices at which funeral goods or funeral services are offered, that price information is available over the telephone.

    (ii) Tell persons who ask by telephone about the funeral provider's offerings or prices any accurate information from the price lists in paragraph (b)(2) through (4) of this section which reasonably answers the question and any other information which reasonably answers the question and which is readily available.

2. Casket Price List.

(i) Give a printed or typewritten price list to people who inquire in person about the offerings or prices of caskets or alternative containers. The funeral provider must offer the list upon beginning discussion of, but in any event before, showing caskets. The list must contain at least the retail prices of all caskets and alternative containers offered which do not require special ordering, enough information to identify each, and the effective date for the price list. In lieu of a written list, other formats, such as notebooks, brochures, or charts may be used if they contain the same information as would the printed or typewritten list, and display it in a clear and conspicuous manner. Provided, however, that funeral providers do not have to make a casket price list available if the funeral providers place on the general price list, specified in paragraph (b)(4) of this section, the information which is required by this paragraph (b)(2)(i) of this section.

(ii) Place on the list, whether a printed or typewritten list or other format is used, the name of the funeral provider's place of business and a caption describing the list as a "casket price list."

3. Outer Burial Container Price List.

(i) Give a printed or typewritten price list to people who inquire in person about outer burial container offerings or prices. The funeral provider must offer the list upon beginning discussion of, but in any event before, showing the containers. The list must contain at least the retail prices of all outer burial containers offered which do not require special ordering, enough information to identify each container, and the effective date for the prices listed. In lieu of a written list, the funeral director may use other formats, such as notebooks, brochures, or charts, if they contain the same information as the printed or typewritten list, and display it in a clear and conspicuous manner. Provided, however, that funeral providers do not have to make an outer burial container price list available if the funeral provider's place on the general price list, specified in paragraph (b)(4) of this section, the information which is required by this paragraph (b)(3)(i) of this section.

(ii) Place on the list, whether a printed or typewritten list or other format is used, the name of the funeral provider's place of business and a caption describing the list as an "outer burial container price list."

4. General Price List.

(i) Give a printed or typewritten price list for retention to persons who inquire in person about funeral arrangements or the prices of funeral goods or funeral services. When people inquire in person about funeral arrangements or the prices of funeral goods or funeral services, the funeral provider must offer them the list upon beginning discussion either of funeral arrangements or of the selection of any funeral goods or funeral services. This list must contain at least the following information:

(a) The name, address and telephone number of the funeral provider's place of business;

(b) A caption describing the list as a "general price list";

(c) The effective date for the price list; and

(d) In immediate conjunction with the price disclosures required by paragraph (b)(4)(ii) of this section [below], the statement: "This list does not include prices for certain items that you may ask us to buy for you, such as cemetery or crematory services, flowers, and newspaper notices. The prices for those items will be shown on your bill or the statement describing the funeral goods and services you selected."

(ii) Include on the price list, in any order, the retail prices (expressed either as the flat fee, or as the price per hour, mile or other unit of computation) and the other information specified below for at least each of the following items, if offered for sale:

(a) Forwarding of remains to another funeral home, together with a list of the services provided for any quoted price;

(b) Receiving remains from another funeral home, together with a list of the services provided for any quoted price;

(c) The price range for the direct cremations offered by the funeral provider, together with: (1) A separate price for a direct cremation where the purchaser provides the container; (2) separate prices for each direct cremation offered including an unfinished wood box or alternative container; and (3) a description of the services and container (where applicable), included in each price;

(d) The price range for the immediate burials offered by the funeral provider, together with: (1) a separate price for an immediate burial where the purchaser provides the casket; (2) separate prices for each immediate burial offered including a casket or alternative container; and (3) a description of the services and container (where applicable) included in that price.

(e) Transfer of remains to funeral home.

(f) Embalming.

(g) Other preparation of the body.

(h) Use of facilities for viewing.

(i) Use of facilities for funeral ceremony.

(j) Other use of facilities, together with a list of facilities provided for any quoted price.

(k) Hearse.

(l) Limousine.

(m) Other automotive equipment, together with a description of the automotive equipment provided for any quoted price; and

(n) Acknowledgment cards.

(iii) Include on the price list, in any order, the following information:

(A) Either of the following:

(1) The price range for the caskets offered by the funeral provider, together with the statement: "A complete price list will be provided at the funeral home;" or

        (2) The prices of individual caskets, disclosed in the manner specified by paragraph (b)(2)(i) [above] of this section; and

    (B) Either of the following:

        (1) The price range for the outer burial containers offered by the funeral provider, together with the statement: "A complete price list will be provided at the funeral home;" or

        (2) The prices of individual outer burial containers, disclosed in the manner specified by paragraph (b)(3)(i) [above] of this section; and

    (C) Either of the following:

        (1) The price for the services of funeral director and staff, together with a list of the principal services provided for any quoted price and, if the charge cannot be declined by the purchaser, the statement: "This fee for our services will be added to the total cost of the funeral arrangements you select. (This fee is already included in our charges for direct cremations, immediate burials, and forwarding or receiving remains.)"; or

        (2) The following statement: "Please note that a fee for the use of our services is included in the price of our caskets. Our services include (specify):" The statement must be placed on the general price list together with casket price range, required by paragraph (b)(4)(iii)(A)(1) [above] of this section, or together with the prices of individual caskets, required by (b)(4)(iii)(A)(2) [above].

5. Statement of Funeral Goods and Services Selected.

    (i) Give an itemized written statement for retention to each person, who arranges a funeral or other disposition of human remains, at the conclusion of the discussion of arrangements. The statement must list at least the following information:

        (a) The funeral goods and funeral services selected by that person and the prices to be paid for each of them;

(b) Specifically itemized cash advance items. (These prices must be given to the extent then known or reasonably ascertainable. If the prices are not known or reasonably ascertainable, a good faith estimate shall be given and a written statement of the actual charges shall be provided before the final bill is paid.); and

(c) The total cost of the goods and services selected.

(ii) The information required by this paragraph (b)(5) of this section may be included on any contract, statement, or other document which the funeral provider would otherwise provide at the conclusion of discussion of arrangements.

6. Other Pricing Methods.

Funeral providers may give persons any other price information, in any other format, in addition to that required by paragraphs (b)(2), (3) and (4) of this section so long as the statement required by paragraph (b)(5) of this section is given when required by the rule.

SECTION 453.3 MISREPRESENTATIONS

(a) Embalming Provisions.

(1) Deceptive acts or practices. In selling or offering to sell funeral goods or funeral services to the public, it is a deceptive act or practice for a funeral provider to:

(i) Represent that state or local law requires that a deceased person be embalmed when such is not the case;

(ii) Fail to disclose that embalming is not required by law except in certain special cases.

(2) Preventative requirements. To prevent these deceptive acts or practices, as well as the unfair or deceptive acts or practices defined in Sections 453.4(b)(1) and 453.5(2), funeral providers must:

(i) Not represent that a deceased person is required to be embalmed for direct cremation, immediate burial, a funeral using a sealed casket, or if refrigeration is available and the funeral is without viewing or visitation and with closed casket when state or local law does not require embalming;

(ii) Place the following disclosure on the general price list, required by Section 453.2(b)(4), in immediate conjunction with the price shown for embalming: "Except in certain special cases, embalming is not required by law.

Embalming may be necessary, however, if you select certain funeral arrangements, such as a funeral with viewing. If you do not want embalming, you usually have the right to choose an arrangement which does not require you to pay for it, such as direct cremation or immediate burial."

(b) Casket for Cremation Provisions.

(1) Deceptive acts or practices. In selling or offering to sell funeral goods or funeral services to the public, it is an acceptive act or practice for a funeral provider to:

(i) Represent that state or local law requires a casket for direct cremations;

(ii) Represent that a casket (other than an unfinished wood box) is required for direct cremations.

(2) Preventative requirements. To prevent these deceptive acts or practices, as well as the unfair or deceptive acts or practices defined in Section 453.4(a)(1), funeral providers must place the following disclosure in immediate conjunction with the price range shown for direct cremations: "If you want to arrange a direct cremation, you can use an unfinished wood box or an alternative container. Alternative containers can be made of materials like heavy cardboard or composition materials (with or without an outside covering), or pouches of canvas." This disclosure only has to be placed on the general price list if the funeral provider arranges direct cremations.

(c) Other Burial Container Provisions.

(1) Deceptive acts of practices. In selling or offering to sell funeral goods and funeral services to the public, it is a deceptive act or practice for a funeral provider to:

    (i) Represent that state or local laws or regulations or particular cemeteries, require outer burial containers when such is not the case;

    (ii) Fail to disclose to persons arranging funerals that state law does not require the purchase of an outer burial container.

(2) Preventative requirement. To prevent these deceptive acts or practices, funeral providers must place the following disclosure on the outer burial container price list, required by Section 453.2 (b)(3)(ii), or, if the prices of outer burial containers are listed on the general price list, required by Section 453.2(b)(4), in immediate conjunction with those prices: "In most areas of the country, no state or local law makes you buy a container to surround the casket in the grave. However, many cemeteries ask that you have such a container so that the grave will not sink in. Either a burial vault or a grave liner will satisfy these requirements."

(d) General Provisions on Legal and Cemetery Requirements.

(1) Deceptive acts or practices. In selling or offering to sell funeral goods or funeral services to the public, it is a deceptive act or practice for funeral providers to represent that federal, state, or local laws, or particular cemeteries or crematories, require the purchase of any funeral goods or funeral services when such is not the case.

(2) Preventative requirements. To prevent these deceptive acts or practices, as well as the deceptive acts or practices identified in Section 453.3(a)(1), Section 453.3(b)(1) and Section 453.3(c)(1), funeral providers must identify and briefly describe in writing the statement of funeral goods and services selected (required by Section 453.2[b][5]) any legal, cemetery, or crematory requirements which the funeral provider represents to persons as compelling the purchase of funeral goods or funeral services for the funeral which that person is arranging.

(e) Provisions on Preservative and Protective Value Claims. In selling or offering to sell funeral goods or funeral services to the public, it is a deceptive act or practice for a funeral provider to:

(1) Represent that funeral goods or funeral services will delay the natural decomposition of human remains for the long-term or an indefinite time;

(2) Represent that funeral goods have protective features or will protect the body from gravesite disturbances, when such is not the case.

(f) Cash Advance Provisions.

(1) Deceptive acts or practices. In selling or offering to sell funeral goods or funeral services to the public, it is a deceptive act or practice for a funeral provider to:

(i) Represent that the price charged for a cash advance item is the same as the cost to the funeral provider for the item when such is not the case;

(ii) Fail to disclose to persons arranging funerals that the price being charged for a cash advance item is not the same as the cost to the funeral provider for the item when such is the case.

(2) Preventative requirements. To prevent these deceptive acts or practices, funeral providers must place the following sentence in the general price list, at the end of the cash advances disclosure, required by Section 453.2(b)(4)(ii)(C): "We charge you for our services in buying these items," if the funeral provider makes a charge upon, or receives and retains a rebate, commission or trade or volume discount upon a cash advance item.

SECTION 453.4 REQUIRED PURCHASE OF FUNERAL GOODS OR FUNERAL SERVICES

(a) Casket for Cremation Provisions.

(1) Unfair or deceptive acts or practices. In selling or offering to sell funeral goods or funeral services to the public, it is an unfair or deceptive act or practice for a funeral provider, or a crematory, to require that a casket other than an unfinished wood box be purchased for direct cremation.

(2) Preventative requirement. To prevent this unfair or deceptive act or practice, funeral providers must make an unfinished

wood box or alternative container available for direct cremations, if they arrange direct cremations.

(b) Other Required Purchases of Funeral Goods or Funeral Services.

(1) Unfair or deceptive acts or practices. In selling or offering to sell funeral goods, or funeral services, it is an unfair or deceptive act or practice for a funeral provider to condition the furnishing of any funeral good or funeral service to a person arranging a funeral upon the purchase of any other funeral good or funeral service, except as required by law or as otherwise permitted by this part.

(2) Preventative requirements.

(i) To prevent this unfair or deceptive act or practice, funeral providers must:

(A) Place the following disclosure in the general price list, immediately above the prices required by Section 453.2(b)(4)(ii) and (iii): "The goods and services shown below are those we can provide to our customers. You may choose only the items you desire. If legal or other requirements mean you must buy any items you did not specifically ask for, we will explain the reason in writing on the statement we provide describing the funeral goods and services you selected."

Provided, however, that if the charge for "services of funeral director and staff" cannot be declined by the purchaser, the statement shall include the sentence: "However, any funeral arrangements you select will include a charge for our services" between the second and third sentences of the statement specified above herein; and

(B) Place the following disclosure on the statement of funeral goods and services selected, required by Section 453.2(b)(5)(ii): "Charges are only for those items that are used. If we are required by law to use any items, we will explain the reasons in writing below."

(ii) A funeral provider shall not violate this section by failing to comply with a request for a combination of goods or services which would be impossible, impractical, or excessively burdensome to provide.

SECTION 453.5 SERVICES PROVIDED WITHOUT PRIOR APPROVAL

(a) Unfair or Deceptive Acts or Practices. In selling or offering to sell funeral goods or funeral services to the public, it is an unfair or deceptive act or practice for any provider to embalm a deceased human body for a fee unless:

(1) State or local law or regulation requires embalming in the particular circumstances regardless of any funeral choice which the family might make; or

(2) Prior approval for embalming (expressly so described) has been obtained from a family member or other authorized person; or

(3) The funeral provider is unable to contact a family member or other authorized person after exercising due diligence, has no reason to believe the family does not want embalming performed, and obtains subsequent approval for embalming already performed (expressly so described). In seeking approval, the funeral provider must disclose that a fee will be charged if the family selects a funeral which requires embalming, such as a funeral with viewing, and that no fee will be charged if the family selects a service which does not require embalming, such as direct cremation or immediate burial;

(b) Preventative requirement. To prevent these unfair or deceptive acts or practices, funeral providers must include on the contract, final bill, or other written evidence of the agreement or obligation given to the customer, the statement: "If you selected a funeral which requires embalming, such as a funeral with viewing, you may have to pay for embalming. You do not have to pay for embalming you did not approve if you selected arrangements such as a direct cremation or immediate burial. If we charged for embalming, we will explain why below."

SECTION 453.6 RETENTION OF DOCUMENTS

To prevent the unfair or deceptive acts or practices specified in Sections 453.2 and 453.3 of this rule, funeral providers must retain and make available for inspection by Commission officials true and accurate copies of the price lists specified in Section 453.2(b)(2) through (4), as applicable, for at least one year after the date of their last distribution to customers, and a copy of each statement of funeral goods and services selected, as required by Section 453.2(b)(5) for at least one year from the date on which the statement was signed.

SECTION 453.7 COMPREHENSION OF DISCLOSURES

To prevent the unfair or deceptive acts or practices specified in Section 453.2 through 453.5, funeral providers must make all disclosures required by those sections in a clear and conspicuous manner.

SECTION 453.8 DECLARATION OF INTENT

(a) Except as otherwise provided in Section 453.2(a), it is a violation of this rule to engage in any unfair or deceptive acts or practices specified in this rule, or to fail to comply with any of the preventative requirements specified in this rule;

(b) The provisions of this rule are separate and severable from one another. If any provision is determined to be invalid, it is the Commission's intention that the remaining provisions shall continue in effect.

(c) This rule shall not apply to the business of insurance or to acts in the conduct thereof.

SECTION 453.9 STATE EXEMPTIONS

If, upon application to the Commission by an appropriate state agency, the Commission determines that:

(a) There is a state requirement in effect which applies to any transaction to which this rule applies; and

(b) That state requirement affords an overall level of protection to consumers which is as great as or greater than the protection afforded by this rule; then the Commission's rule will not be in effect in that state to the extent specified by the Commission in its determination, for as long as the state administers and enforces effectively the state requirement.

SECTION 453.10 MANDATORY REVIEW

No later than four years after the effective date of this rule, the Commission shall initiate an amendment proceeding pursuant to section 18(d)(2)(B) to determine whether the rule should be amended or terminated. The Commission's final decision on the recommendations of this proceeding shall be made no later than eighteen months after the initiation of the proceeding.

Federal Trade Commission
Trade Regulation Rule
(Effective Date: July 19, 1994)*
Part 453: Funeral Industry Practices

SECTION 453.1 DEFINITIONS

(a) *Alternative container.* An "alternative container" is an unfinished wood box or other nonmetal receptacle or enclosure, without ornamentation or a fixed interior lining, which is designed for the encasement of human remains and which is made of fiberboard, pressed-wood, composition materials (with or without an outside covering), or like materials.

(b) *Cash advance item.* A "cash advance item" is any item of service or merchandise described to a purchaser as a "cash advance," "accommodation," "cash disbursement," or similar term. A cash advance item is also any item obtained from a third party and paid for by the funeral provider on the purchaser's behalf. Cash advance items may include, but are not limited to: cemetery or crematory services; pallbearers; public transportation; clergy honoraria; flowers; musicians or singers; nurses; obituary notices; gratuities; and death certificates.

(c) *Casket.* A "casket" is a rigid container which is designed for the encasement of human remains and which is usually constructed

---

*At the time of the 1984 FTC rule, the commission provided of a review process in four years (1988). This revised rule, which is soon to go into effect, is the result of that review.

of wood, metal, fiberglass, plastic, or like material, and ornamented and lined with fabric.

(d) *Commission.* "Commission" refers to the Federal Trade Commission.

(e) *Cremation.* "Cremation" is a heating process which incinerates human remains.

(f) *Crematory.* A "crematory" is any person, partnership, or corporation that performs cremation and sells funeral goods.

(g) *Direct cremation.* A "direct cremation" is a disposition of human remains by cremation, without formal viewing, visitation, or ceremony with the body present.

(h) *Funeral goods.* "Funeral goods" are the goods which are sold or offered for sale directly to the public for use in connection with funeral services.

(i) *Funeral provider.* A "funeral provider" is any person, partnership, or corporation that sells or offers to sell funeral goods and funeral services to the public.

(j) *Funeral services.* "Funeral services" are any services which may be used to: (1) care for and prepare deceased human bodies for burial, cremation, or other final disposition; and (2) arrange, supervise, or conduct the funeral ceremony or the final disposition of deceased human bodies.

(k) *Immediate burial.* An "immediate burial" is a disposition of human remains by burial, without formal viewing, visitation, or ceremony with the body present, except for a graveside service.

(l) *Memorial service.* A "memorial service" is a ceremony commemorating the deceased without the body present.

(m) *Funeral ceremony.* A "funeral ceremony" is a service commemorating the deceased with the body present.

(n) *Outer burial container.* An "outer burial container" is any container which is designed for placement in the grave around the casket, including, but not limited to, containers commonly known as burial vaults, grave boxes, and grave liners.

(o) *Person.* A "person" is any individual, partnership, corporation, association, government or governmental subdivision or agency, or other entity.

(p) *Services of funeral director and staff.* The "services of funeral director and staff" are the basic services, not to be included in prices of other categories in Section 453.2(b)(4) [below], that are furnished by a funeral provider in arranging any funeral, such as conducting the arrangements conference, planning the funeral, obtaining necessary permits, and placing obituary notices.

SECTION 453.2 PRICE DISCLOSURES

(a) *Unfair or deceptive acts or practices.*

In selling or offering to sell funeral goods or funeral services to the public, it is an unfair or deceptive act or practice for a funeral provider to fail to furnish accurate price information disclosing the cost to the purchaser for each of the specific funeral goods and funeral services used in connection with the disposition of deceased human bodies, including at least the price of embalming, transportation of remains, use of facilities, caskets, outer burial containers, immediate burials, or direct cremations, to persons inquiring about the purchase of funerals. Any funeral provider who complies with the preventive requirements in paragraph (b) of this section is not engaged in the unfair or deceptive acts or practices defined here.

(b) *Preventive requirements.*

To prevent these unfair or deceptive acts or practices, as well as the unfair or deceptive acts or practices defined in Section 453.4(b)(1) [below], funeral providers must:

(1) Telephone Price Disclosure.

Tell persons who ask by telephone about the funeral provider's offerings or prices any accurate information from the price lists described in paragraphs (b)(2) through (4) of this section and any other readily available information that reasonably answers the question.

(2) Casket Price List.

(i) Give a printed or typewritten price list to persons who inquire in person about outer burial container offerings or prices. The funeral provider must offer the list upon beginning discussion of, but in any event before showing, caskets. The list must contain at least the retail prices of all caskets and alternative containers offered which do not require special ordering, enough information to identify each, and the effective date for the price list. In lieu of a written list, other formats, such as notebooks, brochures, or charts may be used if they contain the same information as would the printed or typewritten list, and display it in a clear and conspicuous manner. *Provided, however,* that funeral providers do not have to make a casket price list available if the funeral providers place on the general price list, specified in paragraph (b)(4) of this section, the information required by this paragraph.

(ii) Place on the list, however produced, the name of the funeral provider's place of business and a caption describing the list as a "casket price list."

(3) Outer Burial Container Price List.

(i) Give a printed or typewritten price list to persons who inquire in person about outer burial container offerings or prices. The funeral provider must offer the list upon beginning discussion of, but in any event before showing, the containers. The list must contain at least the retail prices of all outer burial containers offered which do not require special ordering, enough information to identify each container, and the effective date for the prices listed. In lieu of a written list, the funeral provider may use other formats, such as notebooks, brochures, or charts, if they contain the same information as the printed or typewritten list, and display it in a clear and conspicuous manner. *Provided, however,* that funeral providers do not have to make an outer burial container price list available if the funeral providers place on the general price list, specified in paragraph (b)(4) of this section [below], the information required by this paragraph.

(ii) Place on the list, however produced, the name of the funeral provider's place of business and a caption describing the list as an "outer burial container price list."

(4) General Price List.

(i)(A) Give a printed or typewritten price list for retention to persons who inquire in person about the funeral goods, funeral services, or prices of funeral goods or services offered by the funeral provider. The funeral provider must give the list upon beginning discussion of any of the following:

(1) the prices of funeral goods or funeral services;

(2) the overall type of funeral service or disposition; or

(3) specific funeral goods or funeral services offered by the funeral provider.

(B) The requirement in paragraph (b)(4)(i)(A) of this section applies whether the discussion takes place in the funeral home or elsewhere. *Provided, however,* that when the deceased is removed for transportation to the funeral home, an in-person request at that time for authorization to embalm, required by Section 453.5(a)(2) [below], does not, by itself, trigger the requirement to offer the general price list if the provider in seeking prior embalming approval discloses that embalming is not required by law except in certain special cases, if any. Any other discussion during that time about prices or the selection of funeral goods or services triggers the requirement under paragraph (b)(4)(i)(A) of this section to give consumers a general price list.

(C) The list required by paragraph (b)(4)(i)(A) of this section must contain at least the following information:

(1) the name, address, and telephone number of the funeral provider's place of business,

(2) a caption describing the list as a "general price list," and

(3) the effective date for the price list.

(ii) Include on the price list, in any order, the retail prices (expressed either as the flat fee, or as the price per hour, mile or other unit of computation) and the other information specified below for at least each of the following items, if offered for sale:

(A) Forwarding of remains to another funeral home, together with a list of the services provided for any quoted price;

(B) Receiving remains from another funeral home, together with a list of the services provided for any quoted price;

(C) The price range for the direct cremations offered by the funeral provider, together with:

    (1) a separate price for a direct cremation where the purchaser provides the container;

    (2) separate prices for each direct cremation offered including an alternative container; and

    (3) a description of the services and container (where applicable), included in each price;

(D) The price range for the immediate burials offered by the funeral provider, together with:

    (1) a separate price for an immediate burial where the purchaser provides the casket;

    (2) separate prices for each immediate burial offered including a casket or alternative container; and

    (3) a description of the services and container (where applicable) included in that price;

(E) Transfer of remains to funeral home;

(F) Embalming;

(G) Other preparation of the body;

(H) Use of facilities and staff for viewing;

(I) Use of facilities and staff for funeral ceremony;

(J) Other use of facilities and staff for memorial service;

(K) Use of equipment and staff for graveside service;

(L) Hearse; and

(M) Limousine.

(iii) Include on the price list, in any order, the following information:

(A) Either of the following:

   (1) The price range for the caskets offered by the funeral provider, together with the statement: "A complete price list will be provided at the funeral home"; or

   (2) The prices of individual caskets, disclosed in the manner specified by paragraph (b)(2)(i) [above] of this section; and

(B) Either of the following:

   (1) The price range for the outer burial containers offered by the funeral provider, together with the statement: "A complete price list will be provided at the funeral home"; or

   (2) The prices of individual outer burial containers, disclosed in the manner specified by paragraph (b)(3)(i) [above] of this section; and

(C) Either of the following:

   (1) The price for the basic services of funeral director and staff, together with a list of the principal basic services provided for any quoted price and, if the charge cannot be declined by the purchaser, the statement: "This fee for our basic services will be added to the total cost of the funeral arrangements you select. (This fee is already included in our charges for direct cremations, immediate burials, and forwarding or receiving remains.)" If the charge cannot be declined by the purchaser, the quoted price shall include all charges for the recovery of unallocated funeral provider overhead, and funeral providers may include in the required disclosure the phrase "and overhead" after the word "services"; or

   (2) The following statement: "Please note that a fee of (*specify dollar amount*) for the use of our basic

services is included in the price of our caskets. This same fee shall include all charges for the recovery of unallocated funeral provider overhead, and funeral providers may include in the required disclosure the phrase "and overhead" after the word "services." The statement must be placed on the general price list together with the casket price range, required by paragraph (b)(4)(iii)(A)(1) [above] of this section, or together with the prices of individual caskets, required by (b)(4)(iii)(A)(2) [above] of this section.

(iv) The services fee permitted by Section 453.2(b)(4)(iii)(C)(1) or (C)(2) is the only funeral provider fee for services, facilities, or unallocated overhead permitted by this part to be nondeclinable, unless otherwise required by law.

(5) Statement of Funeral Goods and Services Selected.

(i) Give an itemized written statement for retention to each person who arranges a funeral or other disposition of human remains, at the conclusion of the discussion of arrangements. The statement must list at least the following information:

(A) The funeral goods and funeral services selected by that person and the prices to be paid for each of them;

(B) Specifically itemized cash advance items. (These prices must be given to the extent then known or reasonably ascertainable. If the prices are not known or reasonably ascertainable, a good faith estimate shall be given and a written statement of the actual charges shall be provided before the final bill is paid.); and

(c) The total cost of the goods and services selected.

(ii) The information required by this paragraph (b)(5) may be included on any contract, statement, or other document which the funeral provider would otherwise provide at the conclusion of discussion of arrangements.

(6) Other Pricing Methods.

Funeral providers may give persons any other price information, in any other format, in addition to that required by Section 453.2(b)(2), (3), and (4) so long as the statement required by Section 453.2(b)(5) is given when required by the rule.

SECTION 453.3 MISREPRESENTATIONS

(a) *Embalming Provisions.*

(1) Deceptive Acts or Practices.
In selling or offering to sell funeral goods or funeral services to the public, it is a deceptive act or practice for a funeral provider to:

(i) Represent that state or local law requires that a deceased person be embalmed when such is not the case;

(ii) Fail to disclose that embalming is not required by law except in certain special cases, if any.

(2) Preventive Requirements.
To prevent these deceptive acts or practices, as well as the unfair or deceptive acts or practices defined in Sections 453.4(b)(1) and 453.5(a), funeral providers must:

(i) Not represent that a deceased person is required to be embalmed for:

(A) direct cremation,

(B) immediate burial; or

(C) a closed casket funeral without viewing or visitation when refrigeration is available and when state or local law does not require embalming; and

(ii) Place the following disclosure on the general price list, required by Section 453.2(b)(4), in immediate conjunction with the price shown for embalming: "Except in certain special cases, embalming is not required by law. Embalming may be necessary, however, if you select certain funeral arrangements, such as a funeral with viewing. If you do not want embalming, you usually have the right to choose an arrangement that does not require you to pay for it, such as direct cremation or immediate burial." The phrase "except in certain special cases" need not be included in this disclosure if state or local law in the area(s) where the provider does business does not require embalming under any circumstances.

(b) *Casket for Cremation Provisions.*

(1) Deceptive Acts or Practices.

In selling or offering to sell funeral goods or funeral services to the public, it is a deceptive act or practice for a funeral provider to:

(i) Represent that state or local law requires a casket for direct cremations;

(ii) Represent that a casket is required for direct cremations.

(2) Preventive Requirements.

To prevent these deceptive acts or practices, as well as the unfair or deceptive acts or practices defined in Section 453.4(a)(1), funeral providers must place the following disclosure in immediate conjunction with the price range shown for direct cremations: "If you want to arrange a direct cremation, you can use an alternative container. Alternative containers can be made of materials like fiberboard or composition materials (with or without an outside covering). The containers we provide are (specify containers)." This disclosure only has to be placed on the general price list if the funeral provider arranges direct cremations.

(c) *Other Burial Container Provisions.*

(1) Deceptive Acts of Practices.

In selling or offering to sell funeral goods and funeral services to the public, it is a deceptive act or practice for a funeral provider to:

(i) Represent that state or local laws or regulations, or particular cemeteries, require outer burial containers when such is not the case;

(ii) Fail to disclose to persons arranging funerals that state law does not require the purchase of an outer burial container.

(2) Preventive Requirement.

To prevent these deceptive acts or practices, funeral providers must place the following disclosure on the outer burial container price list, required by Section 453.2(b)(3)(i), or, if the prices of outer burial containers are listed on the general price list, required by Section 453.2(b)(4), in immediate conjunction with those prices: "In most areas of the country, state or local law does not require that you buy a container to surround the casket in the grave. However, many cemeteries ask that you have such a container so that the grave will not sink in. Either a grave liner or a burial vault will satisfy these requirements." The phrase "in most areas of the country" need not be included in this disclosure if state or local law in the area(s) where the provider does business does not require a container to surround the casket in the grave.

(d) *General Provisions on Legal and Cemetery Requirements.*

(1) Deceptive Acts or Practices.

In selling or offering to sell funeral goods or funeral services to the public, it is a deceptive act or practice for funeral providers to represent that federal, state, or local laws, or particular cemeteries or crematories, require the purchase of any funeral goods or funeral services when such is not the case.

(2) Preventive Requirements.

To prevent these deceptive acts or practices, as well as the deceptive acts or practices identified in Sections 453.3(a)(1), 453.3(b)(1), and 453.3(c)(1), funeral providers must identify and briefly describe in writing the statement of funeral goods and services selected (required by Section 453.2[b][5]) any legal, cemetery, or crematory requirements which the funeral provider represents to persons as compelling the purchase of funeral goods or funeral services for the funeral which that person is arranging.

(e) *Provisions on Preservative and Protective Value Claims.*

In selling or offering to sell funeral goods or funeral services to the public, it is a deceptive act or practice for a funeral provider to:

(1) Represent that funeral goods or funeral services will delay the natural decomposition of human remains for the long-term or an indefinite time;

(2) Represent that funeral goods have protective features or will protect the body from gravesite substances, when such is not the case.

(f) *Cash Advance Provisions.*

(1) Deceptive Acts or Practices.

In selling or offering to sell funeral goods or funeral services to the public, it is a deceptive act or practice for a funeral provider to:

(i) Represent that the price charged for a cash advance item is the same as the cost to the funeral provider for the item when such is not the case;

(ii) Fail to disclose to persons arranging funerals that the price being charged for a cash advance item is not the same as the cost to the funeral provider for the item when such is the case.

(2) Preventive Requirements.

To prevent these deceptive acts or practices, funeral providers must place the following sentence in the itemized statement of funeral goods and services selected, in immediate conjunction with the list of itemized cash advance items required by Section 453.2(b)(5)(i)(B): "We charge you for our services in obtaining: (specify cash advance items)," if the funeral provider makes a charge upon, or receives and retains a rebate, commission or trade or volume discount upon a cash advance item.

SECTION 453.4 REQUIRED PURCHASE OF FUNERAL GOODS OR FUNERAL SERVICES

(a) *Casket for Cremation Provisions.*

(1) Unfair or Deceptive Acts or Practices.

In selling or offering to sell funeral goods or funeral services to the public, it is an unfair or deceptive act or practice for a funeral provider, or a crematory, to require that a casket be purchased for direct cremation.

(2) Preventive Requirement.

To prevent this unfair or deceptive act or practice, funeral providers must make an alternative container available for direct cremations, if they arrange direct cremations.

(b) *Other Required Purchases of Funeral Goods or Funeral Services.*

(1) Unfair or Deceptive Acts or Practices.

In selling or offering to sell funeral goods or funeral services, it is an unfair or deceptive act or practice for a funeral provider to:

(i) Condition the furnishing of any funeral good or funeral service to a person arranging a funeral upon the purchase of any other funeral good or funeral service, except as required by law or as otherwise permitted by this part;

(ii) Charge any fee as a condition to furnishing any funeral goods or funeral services to a person arranging a funeral, other than the fees for: (1) services of funeral director and staff, permitted by Section 453.2(b)(4)(iii)(C); (2) other funeral services and funeral goods selected by the purchaser; and (3) other funeral goods or services required to be purchased, as explained on the itemized statement in accordance with Section 453.3(d)(2).

(2) Preventive Requirements.

(i) To prevent this unfair or deceptive act or practice, funeral providers must:

(A) Place the following disclosure in the general price list, immediately above the prices required by Section 453.2(b)(4)(ii) and (iii): "The goods and services shown below are those we can provide to our customers. You may choose only the items you desire. If legal or other requirements mean you must buy any items you did not specifically ask for, we will explain the reason in writing on the statement we provide describing the funeral goods and services you selected." *Provided, however,* that if the charge for "services of funeral director and staff" cannot be declined by the purchaser, the statement shall include the sentence: "However, any funeral arrangements you select will include a charge for our basic services" between the second and third sentences of the statement specified above herein. The statement may include the phrase "and overhead" after the word "services" if the fee includes a charge for the recovery of unallocated funeral provider overhead;

(B) Place the following disclosure in the statement of funeral goods and services selected, required by Section 453.2(b)(5)(i): "Charges are only for those items that you selected or that are required. If we are required by law or by a cemetery or crematory to use any items, we will explain the reasons in writing below."

(ii) A funeral provider shall not violate this section by failing to comply with a request for a combination of goods or services which would be impossible, impractical, or excessively burdensome to provide.

SECTION 453.5 SERVICES PROVIDED WITHOUT PRIOR APPROVAL

(a) *Unfair or Deceptive Acts or Practices.*

In selling or offering to sell funeral goods or funeral services to the public, it is an unfair or deceptive act or practice for any provider to embalm a deceased human body for a fee unless:

(1) State or local law or regulation requires embalming in the particular circumstances regardless of any funeral choice which the family might make; or

(2) Prior approval for embalming (expressly so described) has been obtained from a family member or other authorized person; or

(3) The funeral provider is unable to contact a family member or other authorized person after exercising due diligence, has no reason to believe the family does not want embalming performed, and obtains subsequent approval for embalming

already performed (expressly so described). In seeking approval, the funeral provider must disclose that a fee will be charged if the family selects a funeral which requires embalming, such as a funeral with viewing, and that no fee will be charged if the family selects a service which does not require embalming, such as direct cremation or immediate burial.

(b) *Preventive Requirement.*

To prevent these unfair or deceptive acts or practices, funeral providers must include on the itemized statement of funeral goods and services selected, required by Section 453.2(b)(5), the statement: "If you selected a funeral that may require embalming, such as a funeral with viewing, you may have to pay for embalming. You do not have to pay for embalming you did not approve if you selected arrangements such as a direct cremation or immediate burial. If we charged for embalming, we will explain why below."

SECTION 453.6 RETENTION OF DOCUMENTS

To prevent the unfair or deceptive acts or practices specified in Section 453.2 and Section 453.3 of this rule, funeral providers must retain and make available for inspection by Commission officials true and accurate copies of the price lists specified in Sections 453.2(b)(2) through (4), as applicable, for at least one year after the date of their last distribution to customers, and a copy of each statement of funeral goods and services selected, as required by Section 453.2(b)(5) for at least one year from the date of the arrangements conference.

SECTION 453.7 COMPREHENSION OF DISCLOSURES

To prevent the unfair or deceptive acts or practices specified in Section 453.2 through Section 453.5, funeral providers must make all disclosures required by those sections in a clear and conspicuous manner. Providers shall not include in the casket, out burial container, and general price lists, required by Sections 453.2(b)(2)–(4), any statement or information that alters or contradicts the information required by this Part to be included in those lists.

SECTION 453.8 DECLARATION OF INTENT

(a) Except as otherwise provided in Section 453.2(a), it is a violation of this rule to engage in any unfair or deceptive acts or practices specified in this rule, or to fail to comply with any of the preventive requirements specified in this rule;

(b) The provisions of this rule are separate and severable from one another. If any provision is determined to be invalid, it is the Commission's intention that the remaining provisions shall continue in effect.

(c) This rule shall not apply to the business of insurance or to acts in the conduct thereof.

SECTION 453.9 STATE EXEMPTIONS

If, upon application to the Commission by an appropriate state agency, the Commission determines that:

(a) There is a state requirement in effect which applies to any transaction to which this rule applies; and

(b) That state requirement affords an overall level of protection to consumers which is as great as, or greater than, the protection afforded by this rule;

then the Commission's rule will not be in effect in that state to the extent specified by the Commission in its determination, for as long as the state administers and enforces effectively the state requirement.

By direction of the Commission.